NEW DIRECTIONS FOR HIGHER EDUCATION

Martin Kramer
EDITOR-IN-CHIEF

Understanding the Work and Career Paths of Midlevel Administrators

Linda K. Johnsrud
University of Hawai'i at Mānoa

Vicki J. Rosser
University of Missouri–Columbia

EDITORS

Number 111, Fall 2000

JOSSEY-BASS
San Francisco

UNDERSTANDING THE WORK AND CAREER PATHS OF MIDLEVEL
ADMINISTRATORS
Linda K. Johnsrud, Vicki J. Rosser (eds.)
New Directions for Higher Education, no. 111
Volume XXVIII, Number 3
Martin Kramer, Editor-in-Chief

Microfilm copies of issues and articles are available in 16mm and 35mm,
as well as microfiche in 105mm, through University Microfilms Inc., 300
North Zeeb Road, Ann Arbor, Michigan 48106-1346.

ISSN 0271-0560   ISBN 0-7879-5435-7

NEW DIRECTIONS FOR HIGHER EDUCATION is part of The Jossey-Bass
Higher and Adult Education Series and is published quarterly by Jossey-
Bass Inc., 350 Sansome Street, San Francisco, California 94104-1342.
Periodicals postage paid at San Francisco, California, and at additional
mailing offices. Postmaster: Send address changes to New Directions for
Student Services, Jossey-Bass Inc., 350 Sansome Street, San Francisco,
California 94104-1342.

SUBSCRIPTIONS cost $58.00 for individuals and $104.00 for institutions,
agencies, and libraries. See Ordering Information page at end of book.

EDITORIAL CORRESPONDENCE should be sent to the Editor-in-Chief,
Martin Kramer, 2807 Shasta Road, Berkeley, California 94708-2011.

Cover photograph and random dot by Richard Blair/Color & Light
©1990.

Jossey-Bass Web address: www.josseybass.com

Printed in the United States of America on acid-free recycled paper con-
taining 100 percent recovered waste paper, of which at least 20 percent is
postcomsumer waste.

CONTENTS

EDITORS' NOTES

Midlevel administrators constitute a significant force within higher education. They play key support roles in the four traditional service areas of the academy: administrative, academic, external, and student affairs. These administrators are in constant interaction with faculty, students, and the public and thus significantly affect the tenor and climate of the entire institution. This important group is, however, virtually ignored in the higher education literature. For many aspiring administrators, this gap in the literature means that there is very little information on which to base career decisions. The goal of this volume of New Directions for Higher Education is to provide profiles and career paths of a variety of midlevel administrators who serve in colleges and universities.

Few children grow up aspiring to be administrators in higher education. Few adults outside of higher education are clear about the many administrative roles and functions that support the academic enterprise. So how then do we recruit? How do we attract new talent to aspire to positions about which they know virtually nothing? Although the promotion patterns among midlevel administrators vary, most are promoted from entry-level ranks. So how do we recruit for the entry-level positions? On most campuses, these positions are most likely filled with candidates who show promise, who have the basic skills needed for the particular position, and whose past suggests that they have the attitudinal skills to get along with others, be dependable, and learn. It is from this pool that we draw recruiters, advisors, program planners, and budget analysts. And ultimately, it is from this entry-level pool that we will select the assistants and associates who will eventually become the directors of advising, human resources, campus life, and budget and planning. The process is one of luck and propinquity; it is rarely the result of planning.

Many universities have master's-level programs designed to train administrators for higher education. These programs typically enroll a mix of new graduates with experience in student government or residence hall programming, employed entry-level staff in need of skill and professional development, and career changers seeking new opportunities. There are few readily available resources, however, that describe the breadth of possibilities available in midlevel administration. And neither are resources available to provide more specific information regarding the roles, responsibilities, skills and training needed for, and career pathways to these various positions. For those seeking thesis topics, it is also difficult to identify research questions that are relevant to career areas that they may be interested in pursuing. The profiles in this volume are intended to fill this void.

The book begins with an overview of what we know about midlevel administrators as a group. Vicki J. Rosser reviews the literature and research available to describe who these administrators are, why they are important to higher education, and how they perceive the quality of their work lives. Following this overview, eleven midlevel administrators profile their area of expertise and provide a glimpse into their professional career path. These eleven authors represent the administrative areas of academic advising, international students affairs, institutional advancement, human resources, information technology, enrollment management, budget and planning, student life and development, business and finance, and institutional research.

Their profiles include descriptions of the primary functions of the unit, including the role played in the college or university; the staffing, including the variety of positions, the necessary education and skills, and chances for mobility; the major functional and professional challenges of the unit; the role played by professional associations and the professional literature available; and the needed research in the field. These professionals then describe their path to the position they hold, including their academic background, their experience and training, and the positions they have held prior to their current position.

Virtually all of the positions represented in the administrative units included in this volume require fairly generic skills; only one or two require specific academic degrees or training (for example, fiscal officers typically have business or accounting degrees but not always; human resource professionals often have degrees in human resource management but not always). When institutions seek to fill entry-level positions in these areas, they are sometimes looking for a particular functional background, but more often than not they are looking for potential. They are looking for individuals who are interested in the field, who have good interpersonal skills and a desire to serve. Many more people would be good candidates for these positions than there are people who know anything about these positions. This volume brings together in one resource the profiles of ten administrative functions; practical, insider information about each career field; and the pathways that worked for these eleven successful practitioners. The volume is intended for those inside and outside of higher education seeking information about career possibilities in midlevel administration in colleges and universities.

Linda K. Johnsrud
Vicki J. Rosser
Editors

LINDA K. JOHNSRUD is professor of education and associate dean for academic affairs in the College of Education at the University of Hawai'i at Mānoa.

VICKI J. ROSSER *is assistant professor of education in the department of educational leadership and policy analysis at the University of Missouri–Columbia.*

1

This chapter provides an overview of who midlevel administrators are and why they are important to academic organizations, identifies those issues that affect the quality of their work lives, and suggests new areas for research on administrators.

Midlevel Administrators: What We Know

Vicki J. Rosser

College and university midlevel administrators are the unsung professionals of the academy—unsung because their contributions to the academic enterprise are rarely recognized and professionals because of their commitment, training, and adherence to high standards of performance and excellence in their areas of expertise. Those in midlevel ranks constitute the largest administrative group within most college and university systems, yet they have little participation in administrative policy decisions and no formal structure of governance. Despite their significant numbers and professionalism, they lack visibility throughout the academy and have been of little concern to educational researchers. The purpose of this chapter is to review the literature and data available on midlevel administrators and provide an overview of who they are, why their role is important to higher education, and what issues affect their professional work lives.

Who Are the Midlevel Administrators?

Midlevel administrators may be either academic or nonacademic support personnel within the structure of higher education organizations. Usually, they are not classified as faculty but rather as a nonexempt, noncontract group of administrative staff. As a result, they rarely have the protection of tenure and are vulnerable to budget cuts. Midlevel administrators typically report to a top-level officer, administrator, or dean. They may be classified as administrators, professionals, technicians, or specialists, and their positions tend to be differentiated by functional specialization, skills, training, and experience.

New Directions for Higher Education, no. 111, Fall 2000 © Jossey-Bass, a Wiley company

Midlevel administrators can also be identified by the administrative units in which they work. Although these units may vary by institutional size and type, *student services* typically includes admissions, registration, financial aid, counseling, advising, and other aspects of student life; *academic support* includes media, library, and learning skills–center services as well as cooperative education; *business and administrative services* includes fiscal management, accounting and human resources, operations and maintenance, information technology, and planning and budgeting; and *external affairs* (or *institutional advancement*) includes public relations, alumni affairs, communication, and fundraising (Austin, 1983, 1985; Johnsrud and Rosser, 1999a; Johnsrud, Sagaria and Heck, 1992; Moore, 1983; Moore and Twombly, 1990).

National data on midlevel administrators are confined to demographic data on their numbers and makeup. The Fall Staff report on postsecondary institutions (U.S. Department of Education, 1995) provides the most comprehensive information on eight occupational categories of higher education employees. Two of them, support-service and technical-paraprofessional, seem to encompass the majority of the positions previously identified as falling under the rubric of midlevel administration (Johnsrud, 2000). These two groups represent 28 percent (526,708) of full-time staff within postsecondary institutions, as compared with 31 percent (508,470) of employees who are faculty and 8 percent (155,053) who are executives or managers. The data indicate that women hold 60 percent of administrative staff positions in public and private colleges and universities. The median annual salary for women in administrative staff positions is $28,651, which suggests that they still lag well behind men in similar positions and institutions, whose corresponding annual salary is $31,524.

Only 20 percent of total administrative staff positions are held by minority members (Asians, Pacific Islanders, African Americans, Hispanics, and Native Americans). Blacks have the highest percentage of representation among minorities, accounting for 11 percent of the total, and tend to be most represented in the support-service areas. Minorities also have lower median annual salaries ($28,837) compared with that of Caucasians ($30,619). Of the minority groups noted in the IPEDS study, Native Americans receive the lowest median annual salary ($27,705), but despite their small numbers in the sample (3,335), they have the highest representation in the support-service areas. Although institutional control, type, and administrative unit may have some bearing on the employment ratios of women and minorities to Caucasian men, they remain underrepresented and underpaid in national comparisons.

The ethnic and racial makeup of midlevel administrators at many colleges and universities tends to reflect student and local community populations more closely than do faculty or senior administrative groups. This is primarily due to the nature of the midlevel positions themselves as well as the institution's hiring practices. For example, senior or top-level administrative positions are more restrictive in nature; candidates are often drawn from faculty or from outside the institution via national or regional searches (Johnsrud, Sagaria, and Heck, 1992; Twombly, 1990). In contrast, midlevel administrators tend to be appointed from among qualified entry-level individuals within the institution, which may provide a more ethnically and racially balanced pool of candidates. Those who have the ability and are willing to move internally to gain career advancement and status rise through the administrative ranks.

Many midlevel administrators are promoted because they emerge as the informal leaders within their work units, display strong interpersonal skills, work hard, have the technical skills to perform well in the position, and are dependable. They do not have, however, career paths that are as well delineated and structured as faculty or most senior-level administrators. Instead, midlevel administrative careers tend to have multiple entry and exit points, with multiple paths between destinations (Twombly, 1990). Although the pathways within their careers are by no means traditional in the bureaucratic sense of an administrative hierarchy, their positions remain vital to the efficient and effective operation of most academic organizations. Midlevel administrators are the advisors, analysts, counselors, specialists, technicians, and officers on whom faculty and students have come to rely and trust. These unsung professionals in the academy are long overdue to be studied and recognized for their significant contribution to higher education.

Why Are They Important to Higher Education?

Midlevel administrators are an essential component of higher educational organizations. They are regarded as loyal, skilled, and enthusiastic about their jobs (Austin, 1985; Scott, 1978). As the largest administrative group in most university systems, they may make up as much as 64 percent of all administrative staff positions (Sagaria and Johnsrud, 1992). This formidable group of administrators can significantly affect the tone, manner, and style of the entire institution, and their daily performance levels can determine the quality of relationships with faculty, students, and the public they serve (Scott, 1978). Midlevel administrators are integral to the institution's spirit and vitality.

The significance of their midlevel role lies in maintaining a balance between their supervisors' directions and delegations and the needs and constraints of faculty, students, and public who require their support and services. For example, these administrators serve as the liaisons to off-campus agents or external suppliers of resources that support the college or university system (Scott, 1976, 1977). Building positive and effective relationships with all people and agencies interacting with the institution is important to midlevel administrators (Johnsrud and Rosser, 1999a). These relationships are also vital to the institution and should be acknowledged and encouraged.

Similarly, midlevel administrators are the frontline personnel whom students initially face when entering the college or university system. How those interactions are experienced may be an important factor in student integration, development, and persistence. More than ever, it is crucial to recognize the critical role of these administrators as they interact and participate with students, faculty, and the public and private sector as well as provide public and community service information. Clearly, midlevel administrators contribute significantly to the structure of the academic organization by serving and supporting the primary functions of teaching, research, and service.

Midlevel administrators are also considered the firing-line managers who have the responsibility to monitor and regulate policies and procedures but rarely have the authority to change, adjust, or develop the regulations they enforce. Despite the classic frustration inherent in their "middle" positions, they are seen as a dedicated and committed group of managers who work long hours, are highly professional and skilled, and have a strong sense of connection to their work (Johnsrud and Rosser, 1999a; Moore and Twombly, 1990; Scott, 1978). Thus, understanding the significance of their place within the institution may provide us greater clarity regarding those issues affecting their professional work lives.

What Issues Affect the Quality of Their Work Lives?

In her review of the limited literature that exists on midlevel administrators, Johnsrud (1996) identifies three areas that seem to be a consistent source of frustration for them: the midlevel nature of their role, the lack of recognition for their contributions, and the lack of career development and advancement opportunities. The first of these issues, their classic middle-management position, is a major source of frustration. Senior administrators determine policy, and midlevel administrators have the responsibility to implement and enforce that policy even though they rarely get to contribute to the decision-making process leading up to it. When students, faculty, and the public they serve question the policy, it is they who then must explain and defend something they had no role in creating. Furthermore, they often receive little cooperation from supervisors and have limited involvement with institutional mission and goals, and their role is often vague and ambiguous (Moore and Twombly, 1990). Their participation in governance is minimal (Henkin and Persson, 1992; Moore and Twombly, 1990), yet expectations of their performance remain high (Austin, 1985).

Even worse for midlevel administrators than feeling stuck in the middle is feeling unappreciated (Scott, 1978). They are asked to provide information to decision makers who do not seem to recognize their skill, background, or expertise. Seeking and gaining recognition for their contribution to higher education organizations is an important aspect in the professional work lives of midlevel administrators. Although recognition is considered a basic human need that should be met within most organizations, clearly the perception is that this need is not being met. Recognition for midlevel administrators' competence includes such dynamics as guidance, trust, communication, participation, confidence, and performance feedback. The research findings suggest that if administrators feel their importance as individuals is recognized and accepted, they will respond by increasing their effectiveness (Lindgren, 1982). Similarly, if administrative values and needs regarding recognition are met, their overall morale regarding their work life is enhanced (Johnsrud and Rosser, 1999a), and they may be less likely to leave their positions (Johnsrud, Heck, and Rosser, 2000).

Finally, a persistent source of frustration is the lack of career development and advancement opportunities (Austin and Gamson, 1983; Bess and Lodahl, 1969; Fey and Carpenter, 1996; Johnsrud and Rosser, 1999a; Moore and Twombly, 1990). Few administrators enjoy the opportunity that faculty have to remain in their positions while advancing through the ranks (from assistant to associate to full professor) with increased salary and status (Johnsrud, 1996). Because mobility is limited or difficult within most academic organizations, it is important to enhance professional growth within the institution. Administrators are interested in improving their ability to do the job they have as well as gaining the skills and experience necessary to take on new and more challenging positions. Thus, institutions should provide such a structure of opportunity to promote professional development and enhance midlevel access to promotions.

Institutions that enhance administrators' career and professional development opportunities, recognize their contributions and vitality, and provide internal pathways to gain access and status within the organization may influence them to remain rather than to leave in search of better working conditions. Despite the importance of turnover among administrative staff, there is little understanding of how social and organizational workplace issues interact to influence behavior and subsequent turnover decisions. More importantly, turnover may reflect the perceptions held by employees regarding their work life. The literature suggests that turnover is already particularly high among midlevel administrators (Blum, 1989; Sagaria and Johnsrud, 1988). Turnover, however, can be both a detriment and a benefit to the institution. It can result in a less loyal and knowledgeable labor force and a greater incidence of behavioral problems, such as absenteeism and tardiness (Brittain and Wholey, 1990). At the same time, replacing experienced administrators with entry-level administrators reduces salary expenditures as well as some of expenditures associated with promotional paths and benefit and pension plans (Johnsrud and Rosser, 1999b). Turnover also provides an opportunity to evaluate current reporting structures and position differentiation. Nevertheless, those issues that influence institutional turn-over, either positively or negatively, warrant further attention. More than ever in these tough fiscal times, it is critical to maximize the use of resources and minimize costs. Attending to those institutional and professional issues important to the work lives of midlevel administrators may ultimately affect their daily performance and behavior and thus the tone and tenor of the college and university in which they serve.

What Research Is Needed?

Since the Moore (1983) study, *Leaders in Transition—a National Study of Higher Education Administrators,* appeared, there has been no national study on midlevel administrators. Instead, much of the recent literature and research on this subject has consisted of case studies. Although critically important, this level of inquiry typically focuses on a particular administrative unit (for example, student services, academic support, business and administrative services, or external affairs), institutional type (community college, baccalaureate, graduate), or system (in other words, on a specific public or private system), often within a given locale or state.

Case studies (although limited in broad appeal) are an important facet of research because they are better able to identify a number of specific issues (such as morale, satisfaction, turnover, and intention to leave) within a given context that may affect the views, beliefs, attitudes, and behaviors of midlevel administrators. How midlevel administrators perceive the quality of their work lives may affect their morale (either positively or negatively) and subsequent behavior. For example, in a systemwide study of ten campuses on midlevel administrators ($N = 1,293$), Johnsrud, Heck, and Rosser (2000) attempt to empirically define and measure such complicated work-life phenomena as morale and intent to leave. Specifically, they investigated how midlevel administrators' perceptions of work life (as manifested in career support, recognition for competence, and relations with external constituents) affected their morale and, in turn, their subsequent behavior or intent to leave their current position.

Measuring organizational processes and examining their effects on particular kinds of outcomes (such as intention to leave) are important to our understanding of the work lives and behavior of midlevel administrators. Case studies make substantive contributions in that they provide a basis for identification and measurement of particular issues that can then be examined in a national context. Expanding the research on midlevel administrators from a local to a national perspective would provide midlevel administrators with the attention they deserve in the academy.

In addition to the need for national research on midlevel administrators is the need to examine the organizational level (individual or group) at which we investigate work life. The level of analysis within organizations has consequences for both individuals and groups. For example, the findings in Johnsrud, Heck, and Rosser (2000) indicate that when midlevel administrators (as individuals) perceive high levels of career support and recognition, their morale tends to be higher, and they are less likely to intend to leave. Similarly, if they are not recognized, their morale may be lower, and they are more likely to leave.

At the group level in the analysis, community college midlevel administrators were found to have better collective morale and less intended turnover than their counterparts at research universities. This collective perception indicates that people share a group as well as an individual view within the same institution. In this systemwide study, however, the findings suggest that midlevel administrative perceptions of morale and intention to leave reside primarily within individuals.

The use and application of such multilevel analyses are a powerful means to define and measure such complex phenomena as, in this case, morale and intent to leave. By acknowledging the multilevel nature of organizational data, we are able to achieve a more refined understanding of those social interactions that exist within individuals and among groups. These analyses hold promise for adding to our knowledge about how midlevel administrators experience and construct meaning from the various issues affecting their professional work lives. It is particularly important to identify and address those work-life issues that may contribute to improved morale and retention of midlevel administrators in higher educational institutions.

Conclusion

Understanding the complexity of midlevel administrators' work-life perceptions (as expressed in morale, for example) is important to higher education organizations because those perceptions ultimately may influence how well they do their jobs and how long they stay at them. The challenge to senior administrators is to support those institutional structures and social interactions that midlevel administrators perceive as enhancing their professional work lives and to rectify those felt to be negative in effect. In other words, the institution's climate and working conditions may well be revealed in the attitudes, behaviors, and performance levels of midlevel administrators.

The goal of this chapter has been to provide an understanding of who these midlevel professionals are; to recognize why they are important to academic organizations; to identify those issues that affect the quality of their work lives; and more importantly, to call for more research on midlevel administrators to bring their careers and issues into the national arena. Based on what we have learned about these unsung professionals in the academy, it is only fitting to focus on their profiles and pathways in academic organizations.

References

Austin, A. E. "Factors Contributing to Job Satisfaction of University Mid-level Administrators." Paper presented at the Association for the Study of Higher Education (ASHE) Annual Meeting, Chicago, IL, Mar. 1985.

Austin, A. E., and Gamson, Z. F. *Academic Workplace: New Demands, Heightened Tensions.* ASHE-ERIC Higher Education Research Report no. 10. Washington, D.C.: Association for the Study of Higher Education, 1983.

Bess, J. L. and Lodahl, T. M. "Career Patterns and Satisfaction in University Middle Management." *Educational Record,* 1969, *50*(4), 220–229.

Blum, D. E. "24-Pct. Turnover Rate Found for Administrators; Some Officials Are Surprised by Survey Results." *Chronicle of Higher Education,* Mar. 29, 1989, pp. A1, A14.

Brittain, J. W., and Wholey, D. R. "Structure as an Environmental Property: Industry Demographics and Labor Market Prices." In R. Breiger (ed.), *Social Mobility and Social Structure.* New York: Cambridge University Press, 1990.

Fey, C. J., and Carpenter, D. S. "Mid-level Student Affairs Administrators: Management and Professional Development Needs." *NASPA Journal,* 1996, *33*(3), 218–231.

Henkin, A. B., and Persson, D. "Faculty as Gatekeepers: Non-academic Staff Participation in University Governance." *Journal of Educational Administration,* 1992, *30*(2), 52–64.

Johnsrud, L. K. *Maintaining Morale: A Guide to Assessing the Morale of Midlevel Administrators and Faculty.* Washington, D.C.: College and University Personnel Association, 1996.

Johnsrud, L. K. "Higher Education Staff: Bearing the Brunt of Cost Containment." In *The National Education Association 2000 Almanac of Higher Education.* Washington, D.C.: National Education Association, 2000.

Johnsrud, L. K., Heck, R. H., and Rosser, V. J. "Morale Matters: Midlevel Administrators and Their Intent to Leave." *Journal of Higher Education,* 2000, *71*(1), 34–59.

Johnsrud, L. K., and Rosser, V. J. "College and University Mid-Level Administrators: Explaining and Improving their Morale." *The Review of Higher Education,* 1999a, *22*(2), 121–141.

Johnsrud, L. K., and Rosser, V. J. "Predicting and Reducing Mid-level Administrative Turnover." *College and University Personnel Association Journal,* 1999b, *50*(1,2), 1–8.

Johnsrud, L. K., Sagaria, M. A., and Heck, R. H. "University Staffing Decisions to Hire or Promote." *International Journal of Educational Management,* 1992, *6*(2), 20–31.

Lindgren, H. C. *Leadership, Authority, and Power Sharing.* Malabar, Fla.: Robert E. Krieger, 1982.

Moore, K. M. *Leaders in Transition—A National Study of Higher Education Administrators.* University Park, Pa.: Center for the Study of Higher Education, Pennsylvania State University, 1983.

Moore, K. M., and Twombly, S. B. "Administrative Careers and the Marketplace: Toward the Year 2000." In K. M. Moore and S. B. Twombly (eds.), *Administrative Careers and the Marketplace.* New Directions for Higher Education, no. 72. San Francisco: Jossey-Bass, 1990.

Sagaria, M. A., and Johnsrud, L. K. "Mobility Within the Student Affairs Profession: Career Advancement Through Position Change." *Journal of College Student Development,* 1988, *29*(1), 30–39.

Sagaria, M. A., and Johnsrud, L. K. "Administrative Promotion: The Structuring of Opportunity Within the University." *Review of Higher Education,* 1992, *15*(2), 191–211.

Scott, R. A. "Middle Management on Campus: Training Ground or Wasteland." *Journal of the National Association of College Admissions Counselors,* 1976, *20*(1), 38–40.

Scott, R. A. "Middle-Level Collegiate Administration in a Period of Retrenchment." *College and University,* 1977 (Fall), pp. 42–56.

Scott, R. A. *Lords, Squires and Yeoman: Collegiate Middle Managers and Their Organiza-tions.* AAHE-ERIC/Higher Education Research Report no. 7. Washington, D.C.: American Association for Higher Education, 1978.

Twombly, S. B. "Career Maps and Institutional Highways." In K. M. Moore and S. B. Twombly (eds.), *Administrative Careers and the Marketplace.* New Directions for Higher Education, no. 72. San Francisco: Jossey-Bass, 1990.

U.S. Department of Education, National Center for Education Statistics. Integrated Post-secondary Education Data System (IPEDS), *Fall Staff in Postsecondary Institutions, 1995,* Mar. 1998.

VICKI J. ROSSER is an assistant professor in the department of Educational Lead-ership and Policy Analysis at the University of Missouri–Columbia.

2

Who advises and how advising services are delivered have been the major questions asked about academic advising in the last two decades.

Academic Advising

Kathryn Nemeth Tuttle

Harvard President Charles W. Eliot is the historical godfather of all academic advising administrators. In 1870 he appointed the first administrator in charge of student discipline and development and initiated the elective system that created the need for advisement about course choices (Rudolph, 1962; Veysey, 1965). In 1876 Johns Hopkins University established a faculty advisor system, and by the 1930s most colleges and universities had developed organized approaches to academic advising (Grites, 1979; Bishop, 1987). And although the huge growth of enrollment after World War II spawned the plethora of student services common on campuses today, academic advising received little attention because it was seen as a faculty function. But as the research focus of faculty, the diversity of the student body, and concerns about student retention increased, so did the need for professional advisors and comprehensive advising systems (Frost, 1991).

Groundbreaking articles by Crookston (1972) on developmental advising and O'Banion (1972) on a five-stage academic advising model changed the face of academic advising in U.S. higher education and opened the door to the professionalization of the field (Habley, 1988). The National Conference on Academic Advising was first held in 1977, the National Academic Advising Association (NACADA) was chartered in 1979, and the *NACADA Journal: The Journal of the National Academic Advising Association* followed in 1981 (Beatty, 1991). Coupled with tumbling enrollments and higher attrition, lack of faculty interest or rewards for advising, and student demands for improved advising, many colleges and universities established advising centers or more coordinated advising efforts in the 1970s and 1980s.

The mission of these advising centers varies by type of institution but focuses on advising as a developmental process akin to teaching rather than as a clerical function of scheduling courses and reviewing degree requirements.

NEW DIRECTIONS FOR HIGHER EDUCATION, no. 111, Fall 2000 © Jossey-Bass, a Wiley company

In this model, academic advising is an integral part of the academic mission of the institution, is student centered and concerned about the student's total educational development, and encourages students to share responsibility for advising (Winston and Associates, 1984; Habley, 1988; Frost, 1991).

For most institutions, retention is a key objective of the advising effort. Research confirms that academic advising, student services that connect the student to the institution, and faculty-student contact can have a significant effect on student motivation, involvement, and retention (Chickering and Gamson, 1987; Noel, Levitz, Saluri, and Associates, 1985; Frost, 1991; Pascarella and Terenzini, 1991; Tinto, 1993; Glennen, 1995). Because retention improves the academic and financial foundations of the institution, most colleges have approved the expansion of advising centers in the last twenty years. In fact, the most recent ACT National Survey of Academic Advising found that in that time period, the percentage of institutions with advising centers has tripled to 73 percent and that 78 percent have a coordinator of campus advising (Habley and Morales, 1998). The centrality of the role of academic advising in U.S. universities and colleges seems secure for the twenty-first century.

Staffing and Roles and Responsibilities

Who advises and how advising services are delivered have been the major questions asked about academic advising in the last two decades. After general advising topics, articles on organizational systems have dominated the *NACADA Journal* since its inception (Gordon and Grites, 1998). ACT's National Survey of Academic Advising, started in 1979, has focused on delivery of advising services and also provides a perspective, across institutional types, of staffing, responsibilities, and organizational models. Across all institutional types, the *faculty-only model* predominates, but its use has declined nationally and is employed at only 15 percent of public, four-year institutions. The popularity of the *split model,* which includes an advising center for a designated group of students, such as those with undeclared majors, with all other students assigned to academic departments, has grown in recent years and is now used by 27 percent of all institutions. It is used at almost half of all four-year public institutions and 30 percent of two-year institutions. The third most common model is the *supplementary model,* in which all students are assigned to a faculty member but a general advising office provides assistance for students as well. This model is used more frequently in private colleges. In addition, the *total intake model* involves staff advising all students for a particular period of time and then transferring them to departments. This creates the opportunity for a large staff of professional advisors and is common in community colleges. Finally, the *satellite model,* in which each academic unit is responsible for its own advising, opens the door for positions across the campus (Habley and Morales, 1998).

Although these models take on unique characteristics in different types of institutions, NACADA identifies only four types of positions in its demographic information: academic advisor, advising administrator, faculty advisor, and counselor (National Academic Advising Association, 1999). (The NACADA membership data are skewed, however, because 24 to 25 percent of members leave blank the questions on role as well as gender, ethnicity, and age.) The early history of the association identified conflicts among faculty, professional advisors, and counselors, primarily career counselors, about "what advising should be, who should do it, and who does it best" (Beatty, 1991, p. 9).

Migden (1989, p. 63) argues that professional advisors are "in the best position to meet student needs" because they understand the needs of undecided students, are committed to the retention of students, are more accessible than faculty, and link students with other campus services. With the growth of advising centers and NACADA, the role of professional academic advisor has been well established and is the common entry-level position. The student populations served vary as do the centers' responsibilities. According to ACT's Fifth National Survey, across institutions, academic advisors in advising centers are most likely to serve undecided (65 percent) and at-risk or underprepared (63 percent) students. Advisors working in community colleges, however, primarily serve all student populations. In order of predominance, with a range of 60 to 41 percent, advising centers serve the following other types of students: transfer, part time, adult, disabled, minority, international, preprofessional, and honors, as well as student athletes (Habley and Morales, 1998). Professional advisors have also taken a larger role in providing services to graduate students in recent years.

Primary responsibilities of advisors include advising on general education requirements, serving as a liaison to academic departments and schools, and maintaining academic records. Almost half of advising centers coordinate orientation programs, train advisors campus-wide, develop campus-wide advising handbooks, and participate in academic policy committees. Fewer than one-third prepare registration materials, evaluate transfer credit, or maintain graduation and degree audits (Habley and Morales, 1998). Other typical duties include assisting students with class scheduling, adding and dropping classes, declaring and changing majors, approving graduation plans, helping those with unsatisfactory academic progress, interpreting academic policies, and referring students to other campus services. Nationally, full-time advisors are assigned an average of 267 advisees and see each one 2.7 times per academic term. Private institutions see students more frequently (3.5 times), and two-year public colleges have higher advisor loads (357 advisees) (Habley and Morales, 1998).

Opportunities for advancement in the field are primarily in advising administration—becoming an assistant or associate director or coordinator or director of an advising center. Some advisors hold the title of senior advisor to indicate a more experienced, higher-level position still primarily focused on academic advising. A NACADA survey found that two-thirds of members found a career ladder to be important, but a majority indicated that a career track was unavailable to them. Despite this lack of advancement opportunity, 95 percent were either satisfied or very satisfied with their work (National Academic Advising Association Task Force, 1987). Because most were attracted to the field because student contact was important to them, and noting the high advisor-advisee ratios, the academic advisor position appears to provide a highly satisfying match for most who enter the field.

NACADA data indicate that 48 percent of the respondents' institutions required a minimum of a bachelor's degree for the academic advisor position, whereas 43 percent required and 80 percent preferred a master's degree. Fifty-eight percent did not require previous advising experience, whereas 40 percent asked for one to three years of experience. Forty-three percent indicated no preference in academic background, whereas equal numbers mentioned a degree in the academic discipline in which one is advising, a counseling degree, or a student personnel degree as being important. Experience in teaching and counseling is often a required or preferred qualification. Academic advising, more than other student services areas, demands expertise in academic areas and is enhanced by teaching experience, so it provides opportunities for those with master's and even doctoral degrees in an academic discipline. For those at the director level, as in many student services areas, the doctorate is becoming increasingly important. And because advising center directors interact much more with faculty than other directors or even supervise faculty who serve in their centers, securing a Ph.D. is vital for credibility.

Women dominate the professional advising field, in contrast to the faculty ranks. NACADA has three times as many women as men who are members (of those respondents who identified their gender). The advising experiences of students in most colleges are probably relatively balanced between male and female advisors, however, because faculty members do the majority of advising. For advising centers, attracting and retaining male staff members may be an issue. The percentages of ethnic minority staff members are also a concern. Of those NACADA members who identified their ethnicity, almost two-thirds are Caucasian, whereas African Americans made up 7 percent; Hispanics or Latinos, 3 percent; and Asian Americans and Native Americans, only 1 percent each (National Academic Advising Association, 1999). The need to increase the number of ethnic minority advisors is clear, especially when the results of research about the advising and career counseling needs of students of color are considered (Wright, 1987; Johnson and Ottens, 1996; J. A. Gordon, 1997).

Major Functional Challenges

ACT's Fifth National Survey describes advising centers in crisis and advising practices that are "hitting the wall" in terms of further positive improvement (Habley and Morales, 1998, p. 65). Noting several disquieting trends since the first survey in 1979, Habley and Morales found that gains in campus-wide advising coordination, evaluation, policies, and advisor training had plateaued. At the same time, advising centers served more diverse student bodies, especially students who are at risk; had fewer contacts with students than faculty advisors; and had "inordinately high advisor/advisee ratios" (p. 64). Yet institutions also saw improvement in goal achievements regarding provision of academic information and development of life goals for students. The unrelenting pressure to serve large numbers of students individually, accurately, and comprehensively is the common complaint of most advising centers.

And the ideal of helping students developmentally through advising practice as opposed to prescribing specific courses and programs of study is largely unrealized. "In the real hours of real days advising often becomes whatever can be done to get through most expediently," comments Strommer (1994, p. 92). "Given the numbers of students for whom most advisors are responsible the goal of helping each individual develop as a whole person shifts to firefighting, problem solving, and—often—prescribing." Academic advisors can be overwhelmed with too much student contact and too little time to provide even adequate advising. Sometimes, technology is offered as the solution to these advising dilemmas, and although it has improved recordkeeping and tracking of requirements, it has also added to the financial and training burdens in advising centers.

Firefighting is a common experience for most advising administrators as well. In addition to time pressures, advising administrators are sometimes in the unenviable position of supervising or coordinating independent-minded faculty advisors while not holding faculty status themselves (Kramer, 1981; Twombly and Holmes, 1981). They must contend with issues of marginality within and a lack of coordination across the university: perceived splits between professional advisors and faculty advisors, between academic advising and career counseling, and between academic affairs and student affairs. And external constituencies, such as parents and alumni, criticize advising with little knowledge of current practices, whereas governing boards, which incorporate retention of students into accountability demands, expect that the advising program will solve all attrition problems.

Major Professional Challenges

Because academic advising and knowledge of a wide range of complex academic programs is one of the technically most challenging positions in the area of academic or student services, training of advisors is a significant concern. Nationally, advising training has become less comprehensive, more individualized, and more focused on factual information than on advising concepts and relationship skills (Habley and Morales, 1998). Comprehensive preservice workshops and graduate-level courses on advising are less common than they were fifteen years ago (Frost, 1991). Yet academic advisors are often called on to combine the best of academic and institutional information and personal and career counseling in one thirty-minute session for 300 students each semester. At the same time, one-third of advisors are not evaluated even annually, and fewer and less comprehensive advising reference materials, such as advising handbooks, and student information sources, such as standardized test scores, are routinely provided to advisors (Habley and Morales, 1998). NACADA's programs, discussed in the following section, offer viable professional development, yet financial restraints often make it difficult to send most advisors to annual conferences.

Recognition and appreciation of academic advising and academic advisors has been a professional concern for decades and is influenced by the lack of rewards for faculty advisors. Less than one-third of institutions formally compensate faculty advisors, and recognition has declined since 1992 (Habley and Morales, 1998). This lack of appreciation colors institutional support for all advisors and keeps salaries low. Fortunately, on a national level, NACADA instituted outstanding advisor, advising program, service, and advising research awards in 1984, and the regional associations, as well as individual institutions, have followed suit in recognizing advising excellence (Beatty, 1991).

Professional Associations and Literature

NACADA has dedicated its efforts to improving advising and advancing it as a profession and has undoubtedly enhanced the professional status and leadership opportunities for all advisors. NACADA's national conference offers excellent opportunities, and the ten regional associations sponsor conferences and newsletters that allow ample opportunity for leadership and networking opportunities closer to home. NACADA also offers fifteen commissions that focus on advising different types of students, such as adult learners, business or health professions majors, student athletes, and students with disabilities as well as on different institutional types, such as two-year and small colleges, and different advising roles, such as advising administration and multicultural concerns. NACADA's national presence also enhances advisors' career mobility and provides a professional basis for movement between institutions. An employment service and the NACADA Internet listserv provides quick access to position openings across the nation.

The need for advising research was recognized at NACADA's first conference, and in 1989 the National Clearinghouse for Academic Advising was established at Ohio State University as a national center for advising research. NACADA institutional research grants and individual research rewards also encourage expansion of advising research (Beatty, 1991). Despite these efforts, a study of articles in the NACADA Journal from 1981 through 1997 found that the number and quality of articles had declined; that general advising topics, administrative structures, developmental advising, and student populations continued to dominate article topics; and that few articles appeared on a topic of increasing importance for the future—technology. In addition, direct research on the impact of advising on student success and the effectiveness of advising practices has been very limited (Gordon and Grites, 1998). Undoubtedly, the dearth of advising research is affected by most advisors' and advising administrators' overwhelming responsibilities and lack of interest and ability as well as by the fact that faculty advisors are much more likely to conduct research in their own disciplines than on academic advising. Nevertheless, the field is ripe for those interested in conducting and publishing advising research, and NACADA and the *NACADA Journal* offer substantial opportunities to do so.

Tips for Those Interested in Pursuing a Career in Academic Advising

Those interested in academic advising should focus on obtaining a master's degree. If the degree is in higher education with a student affairs–student personnel focus, it is important to pursue an internship or graduate assistant position in an advising center or departmental or school advising office. Continuing with academic pursuits, classes, and knowledge of the institution's academic mission is vital. On the other hand, if the master's degree is in an academic discipline, gaining some knowledge and experience in student services areas and student development is helpful. Many institutions need additional advisors for new-student orientation programs, and this is an excellent time for graduate students from all disciplines to volunteer or obtain paid positions and experience. Those obtaining counseling degrees should be sure to take adequate coursework in the area of career counseling and try to obtain internships or graduate employment in campus career centers. Many community colleges look for graduates who have counseling psychology degrees with some career emphasis. Many four-year institutions will look favorably on candidates with teaching experience. Teaching in freshman experience courses is one way for those with student affairs backgrounds to obtain some teaching experience. And if paid advising positions are not available, volunteering or internships are viable alternatives.

Path to the Position

Academic advisors are well versed in helping students clarify their paths to career and professional positions through appropriate educational planning. But they are less adept at clarifying the varied and often convoluted paths in their own professional careers. Academic advising is that unique intersection between academic affairs and student affairs, so it is not surprising that the path to becoming a midlevel administrator in academic advising is broader, and more tortuous, than many other collegiate administrative byways.

Like many women of my generation, a career in teaching—elementary or secondary, not college—was the prescribed path. So I dutifully got my degree in secondary education, despite campus political unrest and women's movement protests that encouraged alternate and more adventurous paths. A woman teaching high school social studies was at a decided disadvantage without football-coaching credentials in the teaching glut of the 1970s. Thus, unable to secure a teaching position in an area where I wanted to live and unwilling to pursue one in isolated rural areas such as the one I fled when I went to college, I found work in a public library. It was work I came to love, and my professional path seemed secure once I completed my master's degree in library science.

Again, economic and political forces redirected my professional advancement. A move to California shortly after the passing of Proposition 13, which greatly reduced funding for public libraries, was less than fortuitous. But a small college where I applied for a library position was willing to consider me for an admissions job. With a small child and a husband to support through professional school, I did not pause to consider my philosophy of student affairs but plunged into the student services field in which I have wandered for almost twenty years.

At the small college where my life as an administrator in higher education began, I had the decided advantage and challenge of undertaking an administrative role immediately and ultimately supervising a wide range of student services. I started as director of admissions and became director of student services, supervising admissions, orientation, financial aid, counseling, and student organizations. I was also the only woman on the college's executive board, which gave me broad preparation in the areas of budget, personnel, and institutional planning.

After wearing many hats at a small institution, I returned to a large Midwestern university to become the associate director of admissions, in which position I supervised a large number of support staff and counseled numerous prospective students and their parents. When the director of new student orientation unexpectedly left, I was asked to assume that post after less than three years at the institution. At this stage in my higher education career, I had interviewed for only one of four positions held, all without a degree in higher education.

While in the admissions office, I decided to pursue a doctorate. My thinking at the time was not necessarily career oriented—I had always enjoyed my academic pursuits, and now that my son was school age, I wanted to get back to the classroom. For a time I entertained ideas of pursuing the field I loved in college—history—but soon realized that only the school of education offered the flexibility of course times and programs compatible with a full-time administrative position and the demands of parenthood. I was fortunate to find a small program in educational foundations in the Department of Educational Policy and Administration that allowed me to pursue my interest in higher education history.

Academic advising was still not an immediate goal, but in my work as orientation director, I planned the delivery of advising during the orientation of new students. Like most large universities, my institution had a faculty-based advising system with no centralization and inadequate advising, particularly for freshmen and sophomores. A university committee, prodded by board of regents' demands for better undergraduate education and concerned about retention in the first two years, identified academic advising as a key issue. I was named to the committee, which called for the creation of a new, centralized advising center for first- and second-year students. I was encouraged to apply for the position of director and was hired, more for my broad knowledge and connection to decentralized components of the university than for any previous, specific experience in academic advising. My prospects improved with the completion of my doctorate and adjunct faculty status with the School of Education. I occasionally teach graduate courses in the higher education program as well as frequently teach the freshman seminar course I developed as director of new-student orientation. This academic thread in my student affairs cloth is essential to my role as an academic advising administrator, because faculty advisors are an integral part of our advising center and because of the continual links with departments, the curriculum, and the academic mission of the institution.

Thus, my path to becoming a midlevel administrator in charge of an academic advising center has been circuitous but not unlike those of others in the field who have combined a background in student services with a strong academic focus or who have come from the faculty side to appreciate the issues of student development and have experience in administration in their academic departments and schools. Academic advising bridges students' life in the classroom with their development and goals outside class. And with the focus on student learning and retention expected to continue into the twenty-first century, the opportunities for midlevel administrators in academic advising are bright.

References

O'Banion, T. "An Academic Advising Model." *Junior College Journal*, 1972, 42(6), 62, 64, 66–69.

Beatty, J. D. "The National Academic Advising Association: A Brief Narrative History." *NACADA Journal*, 1991, 11(1), 5–25.

Bishop, C. S. "Teaching at Johns Hopkins: The First Generation." *History of Education Quarterly*, 1987, 27(4), 499–523.

Chickering, A. W., and Gamson, Z. F. "Seven Principles for Good Practice in Undergraduate Education." *American Association for Higher Education Bulletin*, 1987, 39(7), 3–7.

Crookston, B. B. "A Developmental View of Academic Advising as Teaching." *Journal of College Student Personnel*, 1972, 13(2), 12–17.

Frost, S. H. *Academic Advising for Student Success: A System of Shared Responsibility.* ASHE-ERIC Higher Education Research Report no. 3. Washington, D.C.: School of Education and Human Development, George Washington University, 1991.

Glennen, R. E. "Obtaining Presidential Support for Advising." In R. E. Glennen and F. N. Vowell (eds.), *Academic Advising as a Comprehensive Process*. NACADA Monograph Series no. 2. Manhattan, Kans.: National Academic Advising Association, 1995.

Gordon, J. A. "A Critical Interpretation of Policies for Minority Students in Washington State." *NACADA Journal,* 1997, *17*(1), 15–21.

Gordon, V. N., and Grites, T. J. "The *NACADA Journal* 1981–1997: Fulfilling Its Purpose?" *NACADA Journal,* 1998, *18*(1), 6–14.

Grites, T. J. *Academic Advising: Getting Us Through the Eighties*. AAHE-ERIC Higher Education Research Report no. 7. Washington, D.C.: American Association for Higher Education, 1979.

Habley, W. R. "Introduction and Overview." In W. Habley (ed.), *The Status and Future of Academic Advising: Problems and Promise*. Iowa City: American College Testing Program, 1988.

Habley, W. R., and Morales, R. H. *Current Practices in Academic Advising: Final Report on ACT's Fifth National Survey of Academic Advising*. NACADA Monograph Series no. 6. Manhattan, Kans.: National Academic Advising Association, 1998.

Johnson, I. H., and Ottens, A. J. *Leveling the Playing Field: Promoting Academic Success for Students of Color*. New Directions for Student Services, no. 74. San Francisco: Jossey-Bass, 1996.

Kramer, D. W. "The Advising Coordinator: Managing from a One-Down Position." *NACADA Journal,* 1981, *1*(1), 7–15.

Migden, J. "The Professional Advisor." *NACADA Journal,* 1989, *9*(1), 63–68.

National Academic Advising Association. "NACADA Demographic Information, August 18, 1999." Manhattan, Kans.: National Academic Advising Association, 1999.

National Academic Advising Association Task Force. *Advising as a Profession*. Report no. 3. Manhattan, Kans.: National Academic Advising Association, Oct. 1987.

Noel, L., Levitz, R., Saluri, D., and Associates. *Increasing Student Retention: Effective Programs and Practices for Reducing the Dropout Rate*. San Francisco: Jossey Bass, 1985.

Pascarella, E., and Terenzini, P. *How College Affects Students: Findings and Insights from Twenty Years of Research*. San Francisco: Jossey-Bass, 1991.

Rudolph, F. *The American College and University: A History*. New York: Vintage Books, 1962.

Strommer, D. W. "Constructing a New Paradigm for Academic Advising." *NACADA Journal,* 1994, *14*(2), 92–95.

Tinto, V. *Leaving College: Rethinking the Causes and Cures of Student Attrition*. (2nd ed.) Chicago: University of Chicago Press, 1993.

Twombly, T. B., and Holmes, D. "Defining the Role of Academic Advising in the Institutional Setting: The Next Phase." *NACADA Journal,* 1981, *1*(2), 1–8.

Veysey, L. R. *The Emergence of the American University*. Chicago: University of Chicago Press, 1965.

Winston, R. B., Miller, T. K., Enders, S. C., Grites, T. J., and Associates (eds.). *Developmental Academic Advising: Addressing Students' Educational, Career, and Personal Needs*. San Francisco: Jossey-Bass, 1984.

Wright, D. J. (ed.). *Responding to the Needs of Today's Minority Students*. New Directions for Student Services, no. 38. San Francisco: Jossey-Bass, 1987.

KATHRYN NEMETH TUTTLE *is director of freshman-sophomore advising at the University of Kansas.*

3

The field of institutional advancement includes development, alumni relations, and communications. This chapter focuses on the career path of the development staff in higher education, with reference to the other two fields.

Institutional Advancement

Jeri L. Kozobarich

Poised at the edge of the university, with one foot in the academic realm and one in the surrounding community, advancement professionals promote the mission of the institution. They raise money, communicate with various external constituencies, and link alumni to their alma mater. More broadly defined, "institutional advancement is a state of mind that must pervade all aspects of the institution's life. It is an attitude of optimism and ambition that drives an institution's desire to grow and improve in a competitive environment" (Worth, 1993, p. 5). Everyone at the university, from the newest freshman to the university president, plays a key role in institutional advancement. But in reality, the responsibilities for development, alumni relations, and communications, as well as other related areas such as government relations and public relations, lie in a cadre of professional staff specifically trained in their fields. In the most successful universities, the various components of the advancement staff work together closely with a common vision. In the era of declining resources, the advancement team has moved from a peripheral to an essential role within both private and public institutions of higher education.

Advancement as a Career

In all three advancement arenas, development, alumni relations, and communications, discussion is ongoing concerning the professionalization of the field (Buchanan, 1993; Kelly, 1998; Duronio and Tempel, 1997), with members of each claiming a unique knowledge base, code of ethics, variety of professional associations, education, and training. These three functional areas within advancement are not professions such as medicine or law, but they form definite fields of practice with characteristics of emerging professions. Duronio and Tempel note that fundraising, although a field of practice, can be compared to professions "characterized by the public's highest expectations and standards of ethical behavior, interpersonal relationships, and excellence in performance" (p. 2).

Certain personal characteristics contribute to success in these three fields: a broad and current understanding of the institution, high energy and self-motivation, the ability to communicate orally and in writing, an enjoyment of people, and good common sense. The Council for Advancement and Support of Education (CASE), the primary professional association for advancement professionals in education, reports that nearly one-half of its members are development staff (Williams, 1996). Although this chapter focuses on development, information on careers in other areas of advancement are available through CASE. Another professional organization in the area of communications and public relations is the Public Relations Society of America (see Appendix for Web sites).

Development in Higher Education

Members of a university development staff raise money from the private sector to enhance the university's mission. Because of declining revenue from traditional sources, administrators must find new ways to support the university's teaching, research, and service. Basic operating costs are still covered by government (for state-supported institutions); tuition; research contracts; and entrepreneurial, contractual agreements. The university calls on alumni, other friends of the university, corporations, and foundations to support student scholarships, new campus buildings, faculty research and teaching, and a wide variety of other projects that strengthen the university. University administrators often say that private money makes the difference between adequacy and excellence, allowing the university to go above and beyond mere day-to-day operations. The development cycle begins with priority setting within the institution; progresses through identification, cultivation, and solicitation of donor prospects; and ends with a heartfelt thank-you to donors.

Establishing Priorities. Fundraisers work with university administrators and faculty to identify institutional fundraising priorities because these are the people who know the institution best and are able to create a vision for the future. What are the needs of the university? What academic areas will benefit most from additional investment? Which priorities are likely to appeal to friends of the university? Clearly set and articulated priorities help the development staff focus on the core values of the institution. In addition, involvement of faculty and administrators in priority setting will lead to their involvement in the entire fundraising process.

Identifying Donors. The next step is conducting research to identify potential donors to the university. Alumni are considered prime prospects because of their existing link to the institution. Other individuals, corporations, and foundations are considered if they are located near the university or if they have personal or organizational goals that match those of the university.

Developing a Strategy. The fundraisers, working with faculty, staff, students, and administrators, create plans to involve these potential donors in the work of the university and discover their areas of interest. This involvement often provides benefits to the institution beyond the monetary goals, as people and organizations become advocates and advisors.

Asking for a Gift and Thanking the Donors. At an appropriate point after identification and involvement of the prospective donor, someone from the university asks for a contribution. The person asking may be the development officer, the dean, the president, or a volunteer. Formal proposals are written to ask corporations, foundations, and sometimes individuals for money or in-kind gifts.

One of the most important steps in the development process is thanking the donor. A thoughtful thank-you is the first step in preparing to ask for another gift, thus completing the fundraising cycle.

The Organizational Structure. At a large university, development forms a major and complex unit within the institution that is headed by a vice president. Each college may have at least one development officer housed within each academic unit, responsible primarily for major-gift fundraising. A *major gift* is defined differently at institutions of varying size but usually means a gift larger than an annual gift. In some universities, all development staff is housed centrally rather than distributed throughout the university, and debate continues about the advantages and disadvantages of each organizational model. A centralized model may provide more fundraising for the president's priorities, and staff are likely to have a similar institutional view, whereas a decentralized model affords more support for priorities of the individual units. Fundraisers who are housed in academic units are likely to be more immersed in and better able to articulate the academic mission of the unit.

In either model, the people directly responsible for fundraising are supported by a central development operation that includes offices of research, planned giving, corporate and foundation giving, annual giving, and major-donor stewardship. Each is critical to the overall coherence of college and university development. The central offices set policies and procedures, manage the coordination of prospects, and provide university-wide guidance to individual unit fundraisers.

- *Research* staff maintain records, prepare reports, and identify potential funders.
- *Planned-giving* staff have expertise in wills, trusts, annuities, and other gift-giving mechanisms.
- *Corporate and foundation* specialists identify potential funders in these realms and develop the relationships that may lead to grants for the university.

- *Annual-giving* staff run the mail and telephone programs that broaden the base of donors and bring in many small gifts to the university.
- Stewardship and special event offices ensure that donors are adequately thanked for their gifts.

Operations staff, gift-processing staff, and sometimes major-gift development officers in various regions throughout the country also support the college fundraisers. At smaller institutions, the development process remains the same, but staff cannot be as specialized. They are often required to perform many different functions.

Development as a Career

Although development has a long tradition at many private institutions, most public universities have seen the critical need for fundraising arise only during the last decade. Initially, development functions were not understood or appreciated by the academy, and there may still be pockets of discomfort with the idea that a public university has to ask for and accept money from the private sector (Worth, 1993; Worth and Asp, 1994). As state support for universities has diminished, university administrators find they have no choice but to seek funding from alternative sources. As in the rest of the nonprofit world, public universities find that an ever-increasing percentage of their funding comes from the private sector. This trend poses many questions regarding the mission of land-grant universities, as priorities of the donors may conflict with the public interest of the tax-paying citizen. But the trend toward more need for private donations can be seen as a bonanza for the field of development.

Career Paths. Fundraisers have learned that most money given to a university comes from a small number of people. A broad base of support comes from a large number of alumni and friends of the university, but approximately 80 percent of the money is given by 20 percent of the donors. Therefore, it is not surprising that the personnel budget in large development operations is weighted toward support of major-gift fundraisers.

Because of the complexity of the development operation, there are a number of job opportunities in the field. For major-gift fundraisers, the career path may start in the annual fund, where mail and telephone programs solicit relatively small gifts from alumni. Often the path starts even earlier, with student jobs in the annual fund office. Beginning fundraisers may also work in a college under the tutelage of a more experienced development officer. Some careers begin in research or operations, but the skills for these jobs are often different than those necessary for frontline fundraisers. Some fundraisers at large universities move from related jobs within the same university or move into a large university from a smaller institution. There are rarely entry-level positions at major universities.

Jerold Panas, in *Born to Raise* (1988, pp. 212–213), lists what he believes to be the top ten characteristics of a successful fundraiser: impeccable integrity, good listening skills, ability to motivate, high energy, concern for people, high expectations, love of the work, perseverance, presence, and quality of leadership. Kathleen Kelly (1998, p. 88) cites a 1994 study by Margaret Duronio in which the top five characteristics of a successful fundraiser are given as integrity, honesty, commitment, intelligence, and outgoing personality. Kelly points out that these characteristics would lead to success in any profession and discourages people who are considering a career in development from looking for any right combination of necessary traits.

Most of the current advancement professionals, especially those in development, did not begin their careers with advancement in mind; most come from other educational careers, business, journalism, and the non-profit sector (Williams, 1996) and succeed with on-the-job training and professional development programs (Tempel and Duronio, 1997). Although some development staff become high-level university administrators (vice presidents or even presidents), most remain midlevel administrators and find satisfaction in the varied opportunities available in the practice of fundraising and the management of fundraising operations.

The recognition for a job well done in the field of fundraising is rarely public. Credit for facilitating the largest university gifts is given to donors and university faculty and staff, and fundraisers see this as appropriate. However, good fundraising management finds venues for appropriate internal recognition of staff.

Formal Education for Development. In recent years academic programs have emerged to prepare individuals for careers in development. Three well-known programs are the Indiana University Center on Philanthropy (http://www.philanthropy.iupui.edu), the master's program in institutional advancement at Vanderbilt University's Peabody College of Education (http://peabody.vanderbilt.edu), and the Development Director Certificate Program at the University of San Francisco (http://www.cps.usfca .edu/certificates/fundraising). These examples show the variety of educational models in fundraising schools: Vanderbilt University offers the most traditional degree programs, Indiana University offers traditional degree programs and residential certification programs, and the University of San Francisco offers on-line programs. A number of programs and courses in institutional advancement are also offered around the country, usually housed in schools of public policy, management, or education.

Challenges and Opportunities

Some issues in fundraising are as old and basic as questions of honesty and ethical behavior, and others are as new as use of the Internet and the latest financial-planning vehicle. It is important for professional fundraisers to take time periodically to review the ethics of the field, to look toward the future, and to evaluate what is right and what is missing in the theory and practice of fundraising. Fundraisers need to examine the ethical standards that are relevant to individual practitioners, to the institution, and to the field in general.

Individual Ethics. Both CASE and the National Society of Fund Raising Executives (NSFRE) have clear lists of ethical practices in fundraising, and these are reproduced in various publications and on their Web sites (see Appendix). CASE's Statement of Ethics, adopted in 1985, begins: "Institutional advancement professionals, by virtue of the responsibilities within the academic community, represent their colleges, university, and schools to the larger society. They have, therefore, a special duty to exemplify the best qualities of their institutions and to observe the highest standards of personal and professional conduct" (Council for Advancement and Support of Education, 2000). The code goes on to explicitly list the criteria expected in fundraisers, including truth, fairness, honesty, respect for privacy and confidentiality, respect for the letter and spirit of laws and regulations affecting fundraising, and a commitment to nondiscrimination. The NSFRE Code of Ethical Principles and Standards of Professional Practice, adopted in 1991, is similar in tone and content (National Society of Fund Raising Executives Code, 2000). It is a constant challenge to fundraisers to live up to the standards of the field, and thoughtful professional development tackles ethical issues and gives practitioners the opportunity to contemplate possible dilemmas that might be encountered on the job.

Institutional Questions. Ethics in fundraising goes beyond the personal honesty of the staff. Questions may arise about whether a gift is appropriate for the university. Does it enhance or detract from the mission of the institution? Does the donor want too much control over the curriculum and operations of the university? Do we accept contributions from organizations with questionable characteristics? For example, do we accept money for student affairs from a beer company? from a tobacco company? Do we accept gifts for programs that are not a university priority?

Every year a larger portion of most university budgets comes from the private sector. How will this affect the mission of the university? Will the wishes of the major donors prevail over the mandates established by state government? How will the university change over the coming decades as the percentage of money from private sources continues to grow?

The Fundraiser in the University. Fundraisers are often misunderstood within their own institution. In 1994 Worth and Asp noted, "The traditional view of faculty toward college and university fundraisers has been suspicious and dismissive. To academics, development officers sometimes represent an image that is inconsistent with academic values, and fundraising represents an intrusion of commercial values into the academy that is, at the least, uncomfortable" (p. 13). They go on to note an improvement in the academy's view of fundraisers in recent years because they are coming into the field with more advanced degrees and a more professional approach to the task.

Teamwork has eased many misconceptions. The best university fundraising involves faculty, staff, and volunteers as well as the development officers. Faculty participate in setting priorities and in contacting potential donors. They then no longer think of the fundraisers as magical reservoirs of money but as part of a group effort that is moving toward common goals. To create an environment in which external relations and partnership can flourish, attention must be paid to internal relations. "The institution must be understood, trusted, and appreciated in its own home" (Rowland, 1986, p. 139).

Equity in the Field. As in the rest of society, the field of development is far from ideal in its acceptance and compensation of women and minorities. There has been a feminization of the profession over the past decade, and a majority of advancement professionals (53.6 percent) are women (Williams, 1996). Although the number of advancement professionals from underrepresented groups has increased modestly, the majority, by far, is Caucasian (94.4 percent). Women are beginning to be taken seriously as philanthropists (Shaw and Taylor, 1995) as are various underrepresented groups such as African Americans (Kelly, 1998). But fundraising continues to be primarily a field dominated by Caucasian men. Conry (1998, p. 80), studying surveys of the major fundraising professional organizations, writes, "In the past decade, a number of surveys have documented that women in fundraising have made less money than their male counterparts, and even as their occupational participation increases, pay gaps have persisted." More women than men are entering the field, but more men than women occupy higher positions with higher salaries, and there is a gender gap in pay for similar positions (Williams, 1996; Duronio and Tempel, 1997).

Women and minorities are often encouraged to narrow the salary and opportunity gap by following aggressive plans of action: finding mentors, actively seeking career advancement, taking additional risks, and seeking more professional development (Mixer, 1994). Although these are helpful career strategies, fundraising managers must assume responsibility for equity in the field if change is to occur.

Studying the Field of Development

When Worth and Asp were researching the role of the fundraiser in higher education for an Educational Resources Information Center (ERIC) publication in 1994, they discovered little research extant: "The development officer as a significant player in colleges and universities is a relatively recent phenomenon, and there has been little objective research concerning it. The literature on the subject largely reflects the experiences and opinions of various authors" (p. 1).

This problem of dearth of research has been somewhat ameliorated over the past few years as more academic programs in institutional advancement have emerged. But one problem remains: those who practice fundraising are most often far too engaged in practice to engage in research. Katz (1999) suggests the formation of partnerships between practitioners and academic researchers to enhance the study of philanthropy.

Many authors have created lists of subjects in the field of fundraising that need more research. For example, Brittingham and Pezzullo (1990) suggest three primary areas in need of research: the philanthropic environment, the work and careers of fundraisers, and the management of fundraising. By 1997 Burlingame had created a much longer list of research questions that emerged from a Think Tank on Fund-Raising Research (held in 1995 and co-sponsored by the Indiana University Center on Philanthropy, NSFRE, CASE, and the Association for Research on Nonprofit Organization and Voluntary Action) and that have been incorporated into the research agenda of NSFRE. Examples of such questions are as follows:

- What are the demographics of giving or the community determinants of giving?
- What are the financial and management issues concerning fundraising?
- What motivates donors?
- What is the impact of government and public policy on institutional fundraising?
- Are there equity and ethical issues that need to be considered?
- What makes the area of fundraising a valued profession?

If researchers can be convinced of the interest in and importance of research on fundraising, there will never be a shortage of issues to study. And as private contributions become an ever larger percentage of the budget of academic institutions, there is a greater need for research in philanthropy that will lead to more effective and efficient practice.

A Personal Career Pathway

Before entering the development field, I worked at The Ohio State University in student services, alumni relations, and publications. Already holding an undergraduate degree in history from a small liberal arts college, I received my master's degree in higher education while working at Ohio State. I happened into development by accident (Duronio and Tempel, 1997, p. 21, cite studies reporting that a "surprising number" of fundraisers come into the profession by "happenstance.") While taking a course in institutional advancement, I was recruited into the field, and I realized that development is a logical extension of the work I had been doing in alumni relations and publications; all are part of advancing the institution. I began working as a development officer with no formal training, and I learned by reading, attending conferences, watching my colleagues, and listening to donors. I have advanced through the ranks of Ohio State development staff by moving into more complex and challenging environments, by achieving success in my assignments, and by accepting additional supervisory responsibilities.

I have been in the advancement field for fifteen years, and I find that most of my contemporaries, like me, did not plan to become development professionals. Because fundraising has become so visible and essential for the success of higher education, a number of my younger colleagues are entering the field in a more deliberate way, studying development in a formal setting.

Although my primary responsibility is identifying, cultivating, and soliciting major gifts, I also have a wide variety of additional tasks, including those related to college, development, and university-wide committees and special events. I have done consulting at other universities and in the community, and I find the total picture of a career in fundraising to be diverse, challenging, and a great deal of fun. I still see each day as an opportunity for gaining new knowledge, making me right at home in this university learning community. I supervise and mentor a number of graduate students each year, further enhancing my opportunities for ongoing learning.

I seek opportunities for my own professional development several times a year. Because of the frenetic pace of a fundraising career, it is often difficult to take time for professional development, to make conference presentations, and even to schedule a vacation. But in this career, individuals must insist on taking time to learn new development techniques, to keep current with tax laws and giving mechanisms, to reflect on issues of the field, and to relax.

I stay in the field because finding financial support for higher education is very satisfying work. Student scholarships, faculty chairs, and support for academic programs are all greatly needed in the university, and I have a keen sense of accomplishment nearly every day. I enjoy creating and implementing development plans. Although the hours are long, I enjoy the flexibility possible in scheduling my time, and I enjoy the travel. I enjoy meeting a wide variety of very kind and interesting people who are generous donors to the university. I enjoy meeting corporation and foundation leaders and identifying our common areas of interest and visions for the future. I enjoy working in the academic environment, where the creation of new ideas and knowledge generates excitement.

Looking back over my career so far, planning for the rest of it, and mentoring other staff and students has led me to develop a personal tip sheet for myself and others entering the world of fundraising for higher education institutions:

- Love your institution, know as much about it as you can, and take delight in advancing its mission.
- Be a professional: know the business.
- Take time to reflect on your practice and on the emerging issues in the field.
- Remember that you are part of a team. Join with faculty, staff, administrators, alumni, and others to maximize your fundraising success.
- Be nice to everyone. It is not just the right thing to do, but it can bring unexpected and large gifts to the institution.

- Keep your wits about you. Good fundraising is often merely good common sense.
- Have fun! Fundraising in higher education can be enormously rewarding and pleasurable.
- Be scrupulously honest and value your integrity.

References

Brittingham, B., and Pezzullo, R. *The Campus Green: Fund Raising in Higher Education.* ASHE-ERIC Higher Education Report no. 1. Washington, D.C.: School of Education and Human Development, The George Washington University, 1990.

Buchanan, P. M. "Educational Fund Raising as a Profession." In M. J. Worth (ed.), *Educational Fund Raising: Principles and Practice.* Phoenix, Ariz.: Oryx Press, 1993.

Burlingame, D. F. "Critical Issues for Research." In D. F. Burlingame (ed.), *Critical Issues in Fund Raising.* New York: Wiley, 1997.

Conry, J. C. (ed.). *Women as Fundraisers: Their Experience in and Influence on an Emerging Profession.* New Directions for Philanthropic Fundraising, no. 19. San Francisco: Jossey-Bass, 1998.

Council for Advancement and Support of Education. "CASE Mission and Statement of Ethics." [http://www.case.org, June 2000].

Duronio, M. A., and Tempel, E. R. *Fund Raisers: Their Careers, Stories, Concerns, and Accomplishments.* San Francisco: Jossey-Bass, 1997.

Katz. S. N. "Where Did the Serious Study of Philanthropy Come From, Anyway?" *Nonprofit and Voluntary Sector Quarterly,* 1999, 28(1), 74–82.

Kelly, K. S. *Effective Fund-Raising Management.* Mahwah, N.J.: Lawrence Erlbaum Associates, 1998.

Mixer, J. R. "Women as Professional Fundraisers." In T. Odendahl and M. O'Neill (eds.), *Women and Power in the Nonprofit Sector.* San Francisco: Jossey-Bass, 1994.

National Society of Fund Raising Executives. "NSFRE Code of Ethical Principles and Standards of Professional Practice." [http://www.nsfre.org, June 2000].

Panas, J. *Born to Raise: What Makes a Great Fundraiser; What Makes a Fundraiser Great.* Chicago: Pluribus Press, 1988.

Rowland, H. R. "Building Effective Internal Relations." In A.W. Rowland (ed.), *Handbook of Institutional Advancement.* (2nd ed.) San Francisco: Jossey-Bass, 1986.

Shaw, S. C. and Taylor, M. A. *Reinventing Fundraising: Realizing the Potential of Women's Philanthropy.* San Francisco: Jossey-Bass, 1995.

Tempel, E. R., and Duronio, M. A. "The Demographics and Experience of Fundraising." In E. R. Tempel, S. B. Cobb, and W. F. Ilchman (eds.), *The Professionalization of Fundraising: Implications for Education, Practice, and Accountability.* New Directions for Philanthropic Fundraising, no. 15. San Francisco: Jossey-Bass, 1997.

Williams, R. L. "Advancement's Steady Advance." *Currents,* 1996, 12(2), 8–12.

Worth, M. J. (ed.). *Educational Fund Raising: Principles and Practice.* Phoenix, Ariz.: Oryx Press, 1993.

Worth, M. J. and Asp, J. W., II. *The Development Officer in Higher Education: Toward an Understanding of the Role.* ASHE-ERIC Higher Education Report no. 4. Washington, D.C.: School of Education and Human Development, George Washington University, 1994.

JERI L. KOZOBARICH is director of development at the The Ohio State University College of Education, Columbus.

4

Information technology services are expected to be available in a fraction of a second regardless of how many people use them, and Internet capacity should increase as fast as the community can find new ways to use it.

Information Technology

David Lassner

From basic telephone service to high-speed Internet access, from word processing to the administrative systems that underlie institutional business processes, every member of the higher education community relies on a variety of information technologies each day. Unlike most other support areas, information technology (IT) pervades every aspect of the institutional mission: instruction, scholarship, research, service, and economic development. Literally everyone in a college or university—applicant, student, instructor, researcher, staff member, executive, or alumnus—is affected by the quality of institutional IT infrastructure, services, and support. Few members of the campus community understand all the technologies on which they rely, and many understand none of them. Nobody wants to spend more money on technology and support at the expense of direct support for teaching, learning, and research. At the same time, everyone expects that their computer should never crash and that someone should be there to fix it within minutes if it does. Central services are expected to be available in a fraction of a second regardless of how many people use them, and Internet capacity should increase as fast as the community can find new ways to use it.

Ryland (1989) provides a historic development of technology and its support within higher education. Today, the full spectrum of IT support involves a number of diverse functional areas. Although they overlap to a significant extent, it is useful to briefly describe each because they represent specific, identifiable needs and constituencies in most colleges and universities. These needs may be met by individual support groups, larger units that combine them in various combinations, or by an integrated IT organization.

NEW DIRECTIONS FOR HIGHER EDUCATION, no. 111, Fall 2000 © Jossey-Bass, a Wiley company

Administrative Computing

Administrative computing includes the traditional management information systems (MIS) functions of the institution. Like any complex enterprise, a college or university uses automated systems to manage its financial and human resources. Higher education financial systems tend to resemble other public sector financial systems, with the addition of a contracts-and-grants management component in research institutions. Human resources systems for higher education must include a tenure component for faculty in addition to the usual functions. In addition, higher education also relies on specialized student information systems that are unique to the academy; these systems can manage recruiting, admissions, registration, curricula, course scheduling, student records, student accounts, advising, degree audits, and transcripts.

Academic Computing

Academic computing, the traditional computing-center function, typically involves the provision of general-purpose computing and networking for the campus. Functions include e-mail, Web servers and services, a help desk for answering technical questions, software site license administration, public computer labs, and information dissemination through newsletters and campus-specific documentation. The academic computing group may provide or coordinate training and ongoing assistance with any general or specialized software used in teaching and research, from word processors and spreadsheets to statistical packages, geographic information systems, and supercomputing.

Media Services/Instructional Technology

Media services evolved from the traditional audiovisual centers that supported overhead projectors and screens in classrooms and have since become responsible for the computers, digital projectors, and network connections widely used in the classroom today. This function often includes an instructional technology component that assists faculty with understanding the principles and techniques of effective use of technology in instruction, from pedagogy to hands-on assistance with specific tools. There may also be a production facility in which creative staff develop original media (graphics, video, or Web pages) and professional instructional designers develop course materials with faculty.

Distance Learning

Although in 1997–98 only about one-third of U.S. postsecondary institutions were offering distance learning courses, the percentages were much higher for public institutions and large institutions (National Center for

Education Statistics, 1999). These institutions often provide technical support for distance learning through their IT unit(s). Services may include specialized e-mail and computer conferencing facilities, individualized instructional development support, specialized Web packages that support virtual classroom management, and a capacity for video networking if the institution uses interactive video in its distance learning programs.

Telecommunications

Although telephone service has long been considered a basic requirement, data networking has now joined telephony and electrical power as one of the standard utilities for the operation and management of the institution. A modern campus environment includes a data network outlet in every office, lab, library, classroom, and lecture hall. This outlet must provide access to campus network and information services as well as the Internet. Although telephone service is sometimes managed as an auxiliary enterprise and although video networks (for example, campus cable television systems) may have been developed by a media or audiovisual services unit, their management today is often combined as part of an integrated suite of telecommunications services. Other activities that are sometimes part of IT support include printing and duplication, library information management systems, and hospital information systems if the campus operates a teaching hospital.

Organization

Although one or more of the functions just presented might have been managed together, historically there would have been a different support unit for each of these activities, with its own head reporting to a different level of some academic or administrative chain of command. This model has become increasingly disadvantageous as converging technologies and requirements have created more substantial areas of overlap and reliance among the functions and activities. Examples where traditional support service boundaries are breaking down include the following:

• Voice, data, and video communications all use the same conduit and wiring infrastructure. As video and voice are increasingly digitized, experts expect to see even more convergence, with voice and video being carried over general-purpose data networks (Barone and Luker, 1999). Separation of voice, data, or video organizations tends to fragment compatibility and reduce efficiency.

• Both academic and administrative computing rely on ubiquitous networks and central servers that the campus needs on a twenty-four-hours-a-day, seven-days-a-week basis. Distinct infrastructures for academic and administrative computing not only waste resources but are also confusing to the customer community.

• Helping faculty members create a personal Web page to share their research involves many of the same activities as helping to create a Web page to support a course or helping an administrator create a Web page for a unit. Completely separate Web support teams for academic computing, instructional technology, and administration fragment resources and discourage synergy.

• The boundary between the use of instructional technologies to support a campus-based class and a distance learning class is more a matter of policy than pedagogy or technology. Furthermore, campus-based students increasingly enroll in on-line courses developed for distance learning because of their convenience. So separation of technical support for these applications reduces efficiency and increases confusion on the part of faculty and students.

In short, the incredible dynamism and convergence of digital technologies and institutional applications has all but broken the historical basis for separate organizations for different aspects of technology support. In addition, campuses now expect a seamless customer-focused interface to all these services and facilities. So higher education is increasingly following the path of industry by combining IT support units into a single organization that includes most or all of these separate functions and is headed by a chief information officer (CIO). See Penrod (1990) for an analysis of the emergence of the CIO in higher education.

Staffing: Qualifications, Roles, and Mobility

Each area requires staff with specialized expertise in particular technologies, but some general activities cut across areas of IT support. In addition to basic management skills and excellent written and verbal communications capabilities, as required throughout the academy, the aspiring IT manager should have basic skills in the following areas:

Customer service—Training, ad hoc technical support, dealing with difficult customers, and analysis to understand current requirements and forecast emerging requirements

Administration—Complex purchasing, contract administration, higher-than-average levels of human resource activity, work-order processing, internal and external charging systems, and audit processes

Change management—Environmental monitoring of rapidly changing technologies, identifying opportunities for improvement through new technologies, working with customers to identify which services should be eliminated to free up resources for new priorities, and providing consistent service through ongoing internal and external restructuring activities

IT jobs range from entry-level positions that may not require higher education (computer operator, telephone operator, or clerk) to mid- and senior-level management positions that require advanced degrees in specialized areas (instructional technology, computer science, telecommunications, or MIS). Entry-level professional positions in technical areas generally require a four-year degree in some relevant area, although for positions in areas such as network operations, a two-year degree and appropriate technical certification may be as applicable as a four-year degree. IT staffing tends to have more flexibility than other parts of the academy in acceptance of relevant experience or certification in place of formal education. This is consistent with practice in industry, which is faced with a nationwide shortage of skilled IT professionals (Office of Technology Policy, 1999).

At a technical level, excellent mobility exists between different support activities. For example, a good programmer-analyst can be effective in MIS, instructional technology, or developing software to meet specialized needs in academic computing or distance learning. A strong Web developer can be meaningfully engaged almost anywhere because the Web is rapidly emerging as the front end of choice for all information systems and services.

The transition from technologist to manager is much more complex. The key qualifications of successful technology managers are the general management skills mentioned previously, a good understanding of campus needs and priorities, and technical expertise. Many superb technical staff simply never develop the capacity for technology management or an understanding of the needs of the institution. A generic campus manager who has no understanding of the technologies to be managed will have a difficult time keeping up with rapid changes in the field. Although finding excellent managers who fully understand the needs of the organization and the technologies they manage would be ideal, such people are not only rare but also have a difficult time maintaining their technology edge when they are fully engaged in management. IT managers must be actively supported with specific professional development opportunities appropriate to their personal situations.

The dichotomy between technical expertise and management skills presents one of the most difficult challenges for managers in IT. Managers with strong technical backgrounds may be characterized as just techies, and their effectiveness may thus be hampered by the assumption that they lack a real understanding of the academy and its needs. On the other hand, pure managers may find that their recommendations for technology directions are constantly questioned both internally and externally.

Major Challenges

As Peebles and others (1999) point out in reference to the Red Queen Hypothesis (pertaining to a comment by the Red Queen to Alice in *Through the Looking Glass* by Lewis Carroll), IT managers need to work extremely hard just to stay in the same place. The forces that cause this are new expectations, explosive growth, and rapid technological change without concomitant financial support. In most parts of a college or university, growth rates of 10 percent would be considered substantial, but information technologists seldom have the luxury of dealing with anything that changes so slowly. Academic processes are notoriously ponderous, but technologists are forced to work in so-called Internet time, in which products are replaced every three to six months. Over the past ten years, personal computers of greater complexity have spread from the offices of self-sufficient early adopters to every desk, including those of the least computer-literate members of the community who need the most support. Where people used to come to central computing facilities, today every desktop is wired not only to campus resources but to the Internet. Students, faculty, and staff expect and deserve modern information systems and services comparable to the best that industry can offer. Support is expected twenty-four hours a day, seven days a week as the campus community does its work from campus, from home, and while travelling. And although Internet use continues to double each year, connectivity costs have yet to decrease at a comparable pace. Yet in no institution have budgets or staffing levels increased commensurately with this growth in use and demand, and Graves (1999) points out that the common reliance on one-time funding further limits an institution's ability to meet its needs. So one of the underlying challenges for IT managers as they constantly explore new financial opportunities and means for cost reduction is to effectively manage expectations at the same time. This includes setting priorities collaboratively, explaining them clearly, and delivering on commitments.

The tenth national survey of computing and information technology in higher education, *Campus Computing, 1999* (Green, 1999), asked technology officers at U.S. colleges and universities to identify the single most important IT issue confronting their campus. The top four issues were (p. 3):

- Assisting faculty efforts to integrate IT into instruction (39 percent)
- Providing adequate user support (27.5 percent)
- Financing the replacement of aging IT resources (15.2 percent)
- On-line and distance education programs on the Web (8.4 percent)

Consistent with the previous discussion, these issues arise from new requirements (advanced instructional technologies and distance learning), rapid growth (user support), and financial challenges.

Professional Associations and Literature

Fortunately, IT managers need not face these issues alone. The major professional association for the management of information technologies in higher education is EDUCAUSE. Consistent with trends in campus organization, EDUCAUSE results from the merger of the premiere association for academic computing, EDUCOM, and the principal professional association for administrative computing, CAUSE. EDUCAUSE has an active publications program that includes both monographs and periodicals (see Appendix, p. 116, for list of publications). It holds the major annual conference and trade show for IT in higher education as well as a number of smaller, more specialized and regional conferences. EDUCAUSE hosts special-interest groups and initiatives in specific aspects of IT, organizes management development workshops developed and delivered by leading practitioners, works in partnership with major national and international organizations on strategic initiatives, and sponsors individual and institutional award programs that recognize excellence in the profession.

In addition, many other membership organizations are more specific to individual functional areas. Like EDUCAUSE, they tend to have their own conferences, publications, and membership services that provide in-person and on-line networking opportunities and professional development. Although by no means exhaustive, the following list presents some of the significant organizations serving IT professionals in higher education:

CUMREC—Now affiliated with EDUCAUSE, CUMREC (http://www.cumrec .com) hosts one of the larger national meetings focused specifically on administrative computing in higher education.

The Special Interest Group on University and College Computing—This organization (http://www.acm.org/siguccs) hosts two annual conferences, publications, and an awards program.

The Consortium of College and University Media Centers—This group (http://www.indiana.edu/~ccumc/) hosts conferences and publications to advance the effective use of media/instructional technology in higher education.

The Western Cooperative for Educational Telecommunications—This group (http://www.wiche.edu/telecom) has emerged as a national leader in distance learning through a small but well-respected annual meeting and professional development institutes.

ACUTA—Historically serving administrators of college and university telephone systems, ACUTA (http://www.acuta.org/) has broadened its focus on telecommunications. In addition to the typical services, ACUTA tracks FCC and related telecommunications regulatory issues that impact higher education.

The Corporation for Research and Educational Networking—This organization (http://www.cren.net) has metamorphosed from a network operator to originate an innovative series of on-line professional development seminars that address hot topics in a timely manner.

With the emergence of IT as one of the most important factors in the changing higher education environment, many general higher education organizations such as the National Association of State Universities and Land-Grant Colleges, State Higher Education Executive Officers, the Western Interstate Commission for Higher Education, and the American Association for Higher Education have established task forces, published reports, and set new agendas for understanding the technology issues confronting their institutions (for example, Heterick, Mingle, and Twigg, 1998; National Association of State Universities and Land-Grant Colleges, 1999; Western Interstate Commission for Higher Education, 1998). National associations tend to have the greatest importance in policy at both the national and institutional levels, and alliances among IT organizations, library organizations, and these general higher education associations often shape higher education's technology policy agenda.

Many other organizations for IT professionals serve the IT industry as a whole rather than just higher education. These organizations can be fertile grounds for bringing in new ideas from the private sector. Any local technology organizations or local chapters of national associations may be especially important for professional development; joining or working with these groups can be the best way to learn about local market and regulatory conditions, develop local interpersonal networks, establish operational partnerships, and position oneself for mobility outside of higher education within the region.

Academic IT managers rely heavily on the general technology and management literature. The best sources of professional literature specifically for higher education are the professional associations, especially EDU-CAUSE, which maintains a large library of member-contributed documents along with its own publications. Although formal publications still remain relatively sparse compared with many other areas of higher education administration, conference proceedings are a rich and timely source of information on best practices and are increasingly available on-line. Useful hard data on IT in higher education is scarce. The most consistent, continuing national data collection effort is the Campus Computing Project (http://www.campuscomputing.net), which has administered an annual survey on information technology in U.S. higher education since 1990 and tracks the changes longitudinally.

Tips for Getting into IT

Because IT organizations are large employers of student assistants, a significant number of entry-level professional staff are hired from the ranks of experienced student help who have graduated. Graduate students and others interested in pursuing careers in IT are likely to be welcomed as student assistants, interns, or volunteers by the campus technology support organizations. This can give both the student and the organization a chance to determine their mutual fit in a temporary working relationship. Another way to attract the attention of the support organization(s) is to become a knowledgeable user of facilities and offer constructive (and nondemanding) ideas and suggestions.

Campus managers in other areas who wish to make a shift into the dynamic area of IT will be well advised to learn about the specific functional area(s) in which they are interested and study the relevant underlying technologies. Technologists who aspire to management should take advantage of any formal management training opportunities available as well as carefully observe and learn from both successful and unsuccessful managers in their organization. For anyone interested in this field, the professional development seminars offered by the professional organizations mentioned earlier may be one of the best ways to obtain an insider's perspective on the challenges and opportunities in IT management in higher education.

My Path

I entered IT management through a technical career path. As an undergraduate I took a few computer science classes for fun, and upon completion of a liberal arts degree, I decided that further education in computer science would likely aid me in any future career. So I entered graduate school in computer science at the University of Illinois. I had been working as a student programmer developing computer-based education courseware throughout my undergraduate career, and after my first year of graduate school I was invited to Hawai'i to help the university initiate a major computer-based education project in 1977. I never returned to Illinois and over the next ten years took a variety of increasingly responsible assignments in the University of Hawai'i Computing Center involving computer-based education, academic computing, the emerging campus network, and initial microcomputer support activities. During this time I supervised students and staff in these technical areas, became involved in the university's internal budget process and related legislative deliberations, and completed my master's degree in computer science from Illinois at a distance. In the mid-1980s I entered a new interdisciplinary Ph.D. program in communications and information science at the University of Hawai'i.

My break from purely technical management came when I was asked to serve as project manager for the implementation of a new campus cable television system. This assignment led to an appointment heading a new Office of Information Technology, which had been created to develop the institution's distance learning program using a new statewide interactive television network. This office also had lead responsibility for overall coordination and institutional IT planning. At that time the university had four major technology support units. In addition to the Office of Information Technology noted, the Computing Center was responsible for academic computing and academic networking, the Management Systems Office was responsible for administrative computing and administrative networking, and the Telecom Office was responsible for telephone services and the campus wiring infrastructure. In the process of collaboratively developing the university's first strategic IT plan in the early 1990s, it became apparent that having these four independent support units reporting to separate parts of the institution was not serving the university well. The first recommendation of the new strategic plan was to consolidate technology support, and when this was done in the mid-1990s, I was asked to assume responsibility for all four units as the university's first CIO.

Since that time, one of my major challenges has been building a completely new organization out of the components of the original four units. This has involved consolidating three computer rooms and operations staffs into one, four networking groups into one, two user services groups into one, two instructional technology groups into one, and four administrative support functions into one group. At the same time, our new organization has had to cope with all the pervasive challenges previously noted in an environment of budget cuts in each year of its existence. Along the way I completed my Ph.D., which did not make me any smarter but has helped me earn respect (whether deserved or not) in certain academic quarters. And the doctorate has also enabled me to teach in several departments of the university, which I try to do once a year for personal enjoyment and professional improvement.

References

Barone, C. A., and Luker, M. A. "Role of Advanced Networks in the Education of the Future." In M. A. Luker (ed.,) *Preparing Your Campus for a Networked Future.* EDUCAUSE Leadership Strategies, no. 1. San Francisco: Jossey-Bass, 1999.

Graves, W. H. "Developing and Using Technology as a Strategic Asset." In R. N. Katz and Associates (eds.), *Dancing with the Devil.* San Francisco: Jossey-Bass, 1999.

Green, K. C. *Campus Computing, 1999.* Encino, Calif.: The Campus Computing Project, 1999.

Heterick, R. C., Mingle, J. R., and Twigg, C. C. *The Public Policy Implications of a Global Learning Infrastructure.* Washington, D.C.: EDUCOM, 1998.

National Association of State Universities and Land Grant Colleges. *NASULGC Universities Connecting with the Future.* National Association of State Universities and Land Grant Colleges, Washington, D.C., 1999.

National Center for Education Statistics. *Distance Education at Postsecondary Education Institutions: 1997–98.* Washington, D.C.: U.S. Department of Education, 1999.

Office of Technology Policy. *America's New Deficit: The Shortage of Information Technology Workers.* Washington, D.C.: U.S. Department of Commerce, 1999.

Peebles, C. S., and others. "Modeling and Managing the Cost and Quality of Information Technology Services at Indiana University: A Case Study." In R. N. Katz and J. A. Rudy (eds.), *Information Technology in Higher Education: Assessing Its Impact and Planning for the Future.* New Directions for Institutional Research, no. 102. San Francisco: Jossey-Bass, 1999.

Penrod, J. I., Dolence, M. G., and Douglas, J. V. *The Chief Information Officer in Higher Education.* Boulder, Colo.: CAUSE, 1990.

Ryland, J. "Organizing and Managing Information Technology in Higher Education: An Historical Perspective." In B. Hawkins (ed.), *Organizing and Managing Information Resources on Campus.* McKinney, Tex.: Academic Computing Publications, 1989.

Western Interstate Commission for Higher Education. *Reinventing Higher Education Finance: The Impact of Information Technology.* Boulder, Colo.: Western Interstate Commission for Higher Education, 1998.

DAVID LASSNER is director of information technology services at the University of Hawai'i.

5

Today more than ever, the impact of federal and state employment laws makes it imperative for colleges and universities to have a well-managed human resource function.

Human Resources

Daniel J. Julius

To suggest that the management of human resources within colleges and universities is important is to make an understatement. At least three-quarters of the institutional budgets at most institutions are devoted to faculty and staff compensation. A fully developed institution, that is, one that is sensitive to the needs of all employee groups, demands a comprehensive human resource program. To put it another way, an undeveloped or inappropriately managed human resource function can atrophy and lead to partial or full disintegration of a community and, in the process, damage or destroy the confidence that students, faculty, staff, alumni, and the public had in the institution. Today more than ever, competition for excellent people and turnover rates of specialized staff as well as the impact of federal and state employment laws make it imperative for colleges and universities to have a well-managed human resource function.

The first objective of this chapter is to describe the typical functional areas of human resources in most colleges and universities. The second objective is to profile issues attendant to the development and success of human resource administrators.

The Functional Areas of Human Resources

The essential purpose of the human resource function is to create value for the organization. This is accomplished by recognizing that people are an institution's competitive advantage and that human resources must ensure that policies and practices governing the manner by which people work

The author wishes to thank Thomas M. Mannix (retired associate vice chancellor, SUNY) for his insightful comments.

should be judged by the extent to which they enhance organizational competitiveness. Beyond this overriding concern, human resource practices must ensure that administrative, faculty, and staff employment concerns are addressed on a continual basis. This demands review of human resource policies and procedures manuals with the understanding that the appropriate institutional representatives must be involved in the development, implementation, and evaluation of human resource strategy. The human resource management (HRM) process must be fully integrated, bridging academic and administrative functions and objectives. Above all, human resource administrators must make sure that institutional policies and procedures do not hinder organizational flexibility and responsiveness. Too often, the human resource office is seen as a control function. Although defensible policies are important in this litigious age, it is more important to amend policies that inhibit the teaching and learning environment! The dichotomy between the need to defend institutional practices and the need to bend institutional policies to ensure competitive advantage is ever present.

Within any human resource department, there are typically seven areas of specialization: labor-employee relations, recruitment, professional development, institutional benefits, salary administration, classification and compensation, and systems and technology. The following descriptions are intended to be illustrative of the primary responsibilities of each function and not exhaustive.

Labor-Employee Relations. In institutions where faculty are unionized, the labor relations function is often separated from other human resource tasks. There are many excellent reasons for this division. In a unionized context, labor agreements often drive the HRM function. Where faculty are organized, those responsible for negotiations set strategy and legitimate policy in addition to providing contract manuals, training, and contract administration services to all responsible for managing faculty and staff. Labor relations strategies are reviewed to ensure that related processes and outcomes are consistent with the institution's mission and that the implementation of contracts or unionization itself does not adversely impact educational quality or effectiveness.

Every institution should have a formal office where employees can obtain knowledgeable and timely advice and counsel on employment issues. Members of the human resource staff should be responsible for setting goals that align institutional needs with employment policies; establish and interpret formal policies and procedures for all employment issues, including such matters as performance evaluations, contract renewals, probation, involuntary terminations, layoffs, and related disciplinary actions; and monitoring formal grievance procedures for all categories of employees. Such procedures must ensure due process and safeguard institutional and individual rights.

Recruitment. Fundamentally, an optimal recruitment effort results in the attraction of the most competitive and available candidates. The human resource staff may be directly responsible for the recruitment of certain categories of employees and have only consultative responsibilities for the recruitment of others. In either case, the human resource staff should ensure that recruitment efforts focus on one overarching objective: attracting the types of people (based on skills, attitudes, diversity, and work experiences) that would enhance the institution's competitive position. Beyond that, formal systems are needed to review recruitment policies to protect privacy, equal employment, and civil rights. Faculty and administrative staff must be involved with projecting workforce needs or shortages and developing institutional responses to these needs, but the responsibility for managing the process falls to the human resource professionals.

Professional Development. Human resource professionals are often the primary advocates for and sponsors of professional development that enhances individual growth and upward mobility in colleges and universities. Professional development may include supervisory training or career counseling in the areas of conflict resolution, employee discipline and terminations, and performance reviews, as well as providing opportunities for career advancement in the areas of skill development and internal mobility. The human resources office may also sponsor programs to ensure that administrators and faculty are aware of new information, legal or technical changes in various programs or institutional policies, and federal or state legislation.

Institutional Benefits. All institutional employees must have access to information that enables them to make informed decisions on proposed changes in retirement and related benefit packages and how to best use those benefits as well as access to individuals who can provide advice or counseling to employees on such specific issues as retirement, termination counseling, financial planning, unemployment insurance, and wellness and health programs. The human resource office is often responsible for reviewing benefit programs for cost effectiveness, legality, and market competitiveness. Ideally, the institution has a benefits philosophy linked to the character, culture, and mission of the institution; any new services and programs should be evaluated in reference to this philosophy.

Salary Administration. Human resource professionals manage salary programs and endeavor to guarantee that salaries are determined on the basis of a formal system. This does not preclude a system designed to reward merit or provide cost-of-living raises. Salary administration must conform to applicable labor agreements, legislative policies, and wage and hour statutes. And finally, salary administration includes systematically reviewing salary decisions, monitoring and working with the cumulative consequences of those decisions, and making sure that salary programs are consistent with the institution's competitive stance vis-à-vis its comparator institutions.

Classification and Compensation. The human resource function ensures that the institution has a formal system (and professionally trained personnel to manage the system) by which employees are properly assigned to position categories and compensated on the basis of position difficulty. In nonacademic and administrative areas, job descriptions need to be updated on a regular basis, and the integrity of the classification system must be continuously monitored as well. In academic areas, the absence of appropriate, distinctive categories for teaching positions is common, the theory being that professionals (in this case, faculty) continuously monitor the changes and needs in their disciplines. The formal system of classification should serve to guide administrative and staff employees as they seek to advance their careers.

Systems and Technology. As is the case with all administrative offices in higher education, human resource functions are increasingly utilizing systems and technology to provide HRM information for institutional planning. HRM systems should provide usable data and analysis to facilitate effective decision making, and both the data and its analysis should be available for curricular, financial, budgetary, and related decisions. Human resource systems must be designed to protect employee privacy while providing necessary information to deans, supervisors, and other administrators on a need-to-know basis.

The Current Context and Implications for Human Resource Administrators

A variety of factors external to the academy are forcing institutions to develop sophisticated responses to human resource initiatives being promulgated by state legislatures, the courts, and related federal agencies. For example, no college or university can afford to have its workforce unfamiliar with policies and procedures that address the prevention of sexual harassment in the workplace. Similarly, state legislatures pass laws changing compensation levels or enhancing family and sick leave benefits for all workers, yet little guidance is offered to those who implement these statutes. Indeed, the matter of addressing state and federal legislation in the implementation of human resource policies has become so complex that a new cottage industry of specialized consultants has arisen to address, for example, evaluation of tax pension regulations, executive compensation, early retirement (including nonqualified deferred compensation), defensible job classification systems, negotiation of labor contracts, and the implementation of procedures to investigate employee grievances. Spiraling insurance and health care costs are also focusing attention on human resources.

In this context, the middle manager's role has also become more complex. Sadly, midlevel and senior executives have lost jobs (and institutions have been obligated to pay hundreds of thousands of dollars in legal fees) because of mistakes made by assistant deans or other middle managers in the initial intake and processing of employee or student complaints. Human resources is an area where purely administrative mistakes can result in substantial financial, personal, and legal liabilities.

Unfortunately, human resources is still thought of as a staff function that is tangential to the institution's primary mission. Although this perception has changed in institutions or systems where full-time faculty are unionized or where senior executives realize that the institution's workforce does, in fact, constitute a distinctive competitive advantage, in most colleges and universities the human resource staff still reports to the vice president for business affairs and, therefore, is thought to provide auxiliary services to what is perceived as the academic side of the operation. In my experience, there is still an unwritten (and somewhat dysfunctional) rule that only those with academic degrees can manage academic employee concerns. In fact, the human resource and labor relations functions are sometimes thought of as unnecessary by-products of bureaucratic accretion. Part of the problem stems from the notion among some academic administrators that only they know what's best for faculty, regardless of what labor contracts or federal statutes may say. These sentiments are inflamed when collective bargaining agreements or human resource policies are written and implemented by individuals who have little, if any, insight or knowledge into the work of academic administrators or faculty.

The human resource administrator is often caught in a no-win situation: advised to be client centered and value laden (and instructed that in competitive organizations, the human resource officer should rarely, if ever, say no), he or she is supposed to assist departments and divisions in managing their competitive resources, that is, people. However, what is to be done with the occasional faculty member who dates students or the dean who insists that his or her secretary must be reclassified and made exempt from union membership (because that individual does not like being in the union) or the vice president who insists on ignoring the labor agreement? Depending on the clout of the faculty member or administrator involved, human resource managers may have precious few options beyond complaining to their own supervisor or writing a protective memorandum (in the event that the matter develops into a full-blown lawsuit or grievance, at which point a haughty outside legal counsel will ask incredulously, "How could the human resource office have allowed a situation like this to continue?").

This power imbalance is an institutional fact of life; it dictates that the supposedly nonacademic human resource professional must employ a variety of influence strategies to ensure that good practices with reasonable standardization and legal defensibility are implemented—not an inconsequential feat! Moreover, without a firm grasp of the vagaries of academic decision-making processes, new, corporate vice presidents for human resources, who have just arrived from a national bank or major private corporation, often fail in these positions because they assume they have the requisite authority to advance policy (or to get others to follow procedures).

Skills and Training Needed for HRM
in Higher Education

The first meeting of human resource professionals in higher education took place in the late 1940s, when in the aftermath of labor strife following World War II, the role of global leader (in industry, defense, and ideology) was forced on the United States. Research in human resources and labor relations became a highly sought commodity. During this era, the HRM profession achieved a new status in industry and, to a lesser extent, higher education.

The function itself is now becoming institutionalized in interesting ways. For example, consider the case of labor relations. At present, approximately 40 percent of all faculty and 60 percent of all staff in higher education are organized for the purposes of collective bargaining (faculty unions have been active for thirty-five years) (Julius, 1995). Many who served as the first vice president, dean, or director of labor relations have retired. They were a tough breed who came to academe, by and large, through the legal or business professions or held leadership positions in labor unions. As the labor relations function became more institutionalized, the kinds of people hired changed; for example, the new breed looks and acts more like traditional administrators. Although there may be an approximate set of skills needed, most of the policies, procedures, committees, and so on are in place, as are relationships with individuals in external governmental, state, or related federal agencies. A different set of skills and behaviors may be needed to negotiate the tenth successor agreement as opposed to the first labor contract.

The human resource function may be growing more complex, particularly in the areas of compensation, retirement and pension benefits planning, interpreting federal legislation, and so on; at the same time, it is my experience that nontraditional candidates are being hired for such administrative posts. Finding human resource administrators can be a problem because very few programs have been established to train or educate human resource professionals for higher education. There are, to the best of this author's knowledge, few commonly accepted standard professional practices, codes of behavior, or programs where one might go to learn what these folks actually do! The professional associations representing these individuals have failed to develop an agreed-upon set of attributes, behaviors, or skills needed for success. In fact, worthwhile publications and related literature designed solely for practitioners in higher education are rare.

In the human resource area, the technical skills and field knowledge required are obtained either on the job or in business and law schools (where human resources is often only one of many minor concentrations). Few higher education programs have faculty possessing credentials or experience (or an interest) in human resources (the exception, of course, being academic matters related to the work [tenure] of faculty, which, although extremely important given the role of our institutions, constitutes only one element of the knowledge base needed in human resources). Even those departmental faculty who are themselves former senior executives rarely ascended an institutional hierarchy as human resource professionals per se. In fact, most were able to ascend precisely because they astutely distanced themselves from these functions, which are often considered adversarial or nonacademic and hence not related to the institution's primary mission. Unfortunately, the major associations that promote professional development and continuing education for human resource practitioners in higher education rarely focus on issues commonly faced by faculty or academic administrators. Here, too, the abyss between the academic and nonacademic is not being bridged.

In the absence of human resource administrators with higher education experience, colleges and universities must decide whether to seek experienced human resource professionals outside higher education or train higher education administrators in the intricacies of the human resource world. Although either approach can work, there appears to be no preferred path. Both approaches take time. Acclimating an outsider to the nuances of academic decision making and, more importantly, academic politics does not happen overnight. As time-consuming as that approach may be, a good on-campus mentor can work wonders. Learning the human resource ropes often requires substantial legal advice and assistance. A college or university may not have the luxury of time as human resource decisions made or not made can quickly put an institution at substantial risk. A glance at the top 100 schools listed in the latest issue of *U.S. News and World Report* or conversations with national search consultants seeking individuals to fill senior human resource positions reveals a predisposition toward nontraditional candidates with experience in nonacademic sectors.

This is interesting because at precisely the time when human resources is becoming a more demanding area internally (where one has to influence traditional academic types to observe institutional policies and procedures), individuals being appointed may be at an unfair disadvantage if they are perceived as nontraditional or nonacademic hires and, therefore, lack the status and legitimacy needed to influence the more purely academic side of the institution. One result is that many of these excellent and talented new people literally give up and leave.

Building a Career in Higher Education Human Resources

It is not feasible to prescribe one set of attributes, skills, and experiences that will guarantee a pathway to success in any field or endeavor, particularly human resources. That being said, I think it is reasonable to assume that if you are under five feet tall, your chances of playing professional basketball are slim. Likewise, those who fail to appreciate the social and political nature of colleges and universities, are averse to conflict, or lack certain technical skills and credentials will not be influential or effective human resource administrators. I offer the following recommendations to individuals who desire a career in human resources or seek to make the function more efficient and effective.

• *Get credentialed and experienced.* The world of human resources is becoming more complex. Effectiveness demands mastery of technical competencies. Administrative mobility, within and between institutions, is the means by which individuals accumulate skills, knowledge, and experience. In addition, credentials and degrees are of obvious importance in an academic work setting. At the present time, the skills and knowledge needed to succeed in this field are offered on the job or in business and law schools. Hopefully, in the future programs in human resource management for higher education will be developed for practitioners.

• *Professional relationships with supervisors and colleagues must be maintained.* Human resource administrators must know, when push comes to shove, that their words and actions will be upheld and defended. But this will occur only with the understanding and support of supervisors and colleagues. Although it is said that the truth, by its very nature, will persuade, it is important for human resource administrators not only to be right but also to not end up with their head on the end of a stick!

• *Develop strategies and programs that will enable the president, senior academic administrators, and faculty to transcend the perception that human resource interests are not faculty concerns.* Human resource specialists must develop meaningful coalitions and relationships with academic administrators and faculty. (So should their professional associations.) This can be accomplished through enhancing the service function of the human resource office, paying attention to social networks, and developing and refining programs or policies that work and are of particular concern to academic personnel.

• *Reexamine rules and procedures that create the need for exceptions.* Personnel manuals or labor contracts may well be outdated or dysfunctional. In such instances, the documents should be reexamined or rewritten, preferably by a committee empowered for the purpose. An outmoded procedure or clause in a labor agreement should be modified or dropped lest individuals begin to doubt the utility of the entire policy or manual. Does the possibility also exist of survival without any procedure at all? Sometimes people function more effectively if permitted to use their own judgment. You probably do!

The college and university provides one of the most dynamic and stimulating environments for human resource professionals. The rewards for being successful (and the pitfalls for failure) are numerous and all-encompassing.

My Path

I believe that luck, ambition, intelligence, a good mentor, and obsessive-compulsive behaviors are a real plus for aspiring human resource professionals. Moreover, the key to being a successful administrator in a college or university environment is to understand that the manner by which a task is accomplished is as important as what one actually does. It is also essential to possess a particular set of competencies, to attend to your work performance, to network, to manage rather than ignore conflict, to understand how to navigate in highly politicized organizations, to never forget to whom you report, and to endeavor to treat others with respect and dignity. Bear in mind that successful people are those who keep doing the things that brought them success in the first place!

My career path has not been traditional but has been characterized by a determination to achieve and a willingness to network, volunteer, take risks, change locations, and make unpopular decisions. Above all, my stature as a human resource professional has been enhanced by strong linkages to the teaching and research function. I completed a bachelor's degree in the humanities at The Ohio State University and then spent a year traveling Europe and working as a plumber on an Israeli kibbutz. I returned to Columbia University and earned master's and doctoral degrees in the history of education, organizational behavior, and industrial labor relations from its Schools of Business and Education. I began teaching at Columbia, studied industrial relations at Cornell University, and worked as a volunteer at the National Center for the Study of Collective Bargaining in Higher Education at Bernard M. Baruch College, City University of New York. I accepted a position with a management consulting firm in New York City and later moved to assume a post as director of personnel services for the Vermont State College System. I volunteered for numerous assignments and became active in two national associations—the College and University Personnel Association and the Association of Academic Personnel Administrators. (I was elected president of both organizations.) I moved to the California State University System to become system-wide director of employee relations and then assistant vice chancellor of faculty and staff relations. Following this, I accepted a new position, associate vice president for academic affairs and labor relations, at the University of San Francisco. I work as a consultant, continue to teach, and regularly accept invitations to lecture and consult in Europe, Canada, Asia, Australia, the Middle East, and the Persian Gulf.

Reference

Julius, D. J. (ed.). *Managing the Industrial Labor Relations Process in Higher Education.* Washington, D.C.: College and University Personnel Association, 1995.

Additional Resources

Julius, D. J., Baldridge, J. V., and Pfeffer, J. "Determinants of Administrative Effectiveness: Why Some Academic Leaders Are More Influential and Effective Than Others." *Canadian Society for the Study of Higher Education Professional File*, no. 19, University of Manitoba 1999.

Julius, D. J., Baldridge, J. V., and Pfeffer, J. "A Memo from Machiavelli." *Journal of Higher Education*, 1999, 70(2), 113–133.

Julius, D. J. (ed.), *Managing the Industrial Labor Relations Process in Higher Education*. Washington, D.C.: College and University Personnel Association, 1995.

Julius, D. J., Baldridge, J. V., and Pfeffer, J. *The Principled Use of Power and Influence in Higher Education*. Baltimore, Md.: Johns Hopkins University Press, forthcoming.

Julius, D. J. "The Evolution of the Human Resource Function in the American Church Related College." In B. Nicholson-Brown (ed.), *Human Resource Management in Religiously Affiliated Institutions*, Washington, D.C.: College and University Personnel Association, 1991.

Pfeffer, J., *New Directions for Organization Theory: Problems and Prospects*. New York: Oxford University Press, 1997.

Pfeffer, J., *The Human Equation*. Boston, Mass.: Harvard Business School Press, 1996.

Pfeffer, J., *Competitive Advantage Through People*. Boston, Mass.: Harvard Business School Press, 1996.

Ulrich, D. *Human Resource Champions*. Boston, Mass.: Harvard Business School Press, 1997.

White, G. *Profiles of Success in Human Resources*. Washington, D.C.: College and University Personnel Association, 1990.

DANIEL J. JULIUS is associate vice president for academic affairs and labor relations at the University of San Francisco. He is also a senior lecturer in the Graduate Schools of Business and Education at Stanford University.

6

Core duties of international student affairs personnel generally include ensuring a smooth transition into a different educational system, providing ongoing support in cross-cultural and academic adjustment, offering social outlets and leadership opportunities through cocurricular programming, and advising on matters relating to student visa status.

International Student Affairs

Melinda Wood, Parandeh Kia

Working in international student affairs definitely offers one a window on the world. Few professionals in the field get to travel abroad as much as they would like, but the world comes to them on a daily basis. After awhile it becomes routine to receive exotic gifts at new student orientation and to listen to foreign accents every day. It also brings world events into sharp focus when students recount personal stories about losing loved ones in an earthquake, being unable to pay their tuition since their country's economy collapsed, or grieving for friends who have been imprisoned for their political beliefs. Incidents that make riveting news are not just stories; they often create crises for administrators who deal with international students in the United States and with U.S. students studying abroad.

Primary Functions

Many institutions are keenly interested in internationalizing their campuses by making substantive commitment to various aspects of international education. Implementation of this goal can take many forms, such as infusing international perspectives in the curriculum, committing to send U.S. students abroad as part of their degree requirements, working to increase the numbers of incoming foreign students, and creating opportunities for international research. Depending on institutional plans, priorities, and organizational structure, the administrative units charged with meeting specific internationalization objectives are organized in numerous ways.

The most commonly used names for these administrative areas include *international education* or *international student affairs* in their titles; these terms will be used interchangeably in this chapter, though they may not

NEW DIRECTIONS FOR HIGHER EDUCATION, no. 111, Fall 2000 © Jossey-Bass, a Wiley company

mean the same thing on all campuses. These units may be placed within any number of institutional structures. For instance, a unit called Office of International Education or Center for International Student Affairs may be housed in Student Affairs and may encompass both U.S. students going abroad and students coming from other countries to study in the United States. Quite often in this model, these two functions are separated into two smaller units. In other instances, services for international students are located in Student Affairs, and education abroad is located in Academic Affairs. Depending on the size and type of institution, these offices may also be found in the graduate division, the admissions office, or an academic department. For the purposes of this chapter, we will focus primarily on units that serve students coming to the United States because that has been the specific career path of both authors. However, realizing that nearly equal numbers of midlevel administrators work with U.S. students going abroad, we will address issues of both career paths because there are points of divergence as well as convergence.

The functions of these units can vary widely. Their core purposes generally include ensuring a smooth transition into a different educational system, providing ongoing support in cross-cultural and academic adjustment, offering social outlets and leadership opportunities through cocurricular programming, and advising on matters relating to student visa status. On the study-abroad side, additional attention is given to recruiting students and assisting them in selecting an institution in the country of choice, whereas those who work with international students are spending increasing amounts of time on monitoring immigration policy and student compliance.

In 1998–99 over 490,000 international students were attending U.S. colleges and universities, making up approximately 3 percent of all students in U.S. higher education that year (Davis, 1999). Contrary to the popular view that they take resources away from U.S. students, it has been estimated that international students contribute roughly $11 billion to the U.S. economy, making international education the nation's fifth largest service sector export (NAFSA: Association of International Educators, 2000). The majority of students coming to the United States are from Asian countries; are male; and are studying business, engineering, or sciences. Nearly half intend to obtain undergraduate degrees, whereas 43 percent are seeking graduate degrees. In contrast, just over 113,000 U.S. college and university students go abroad to study. They are overwhelmingly Caucasian and female; most go to Western European countries for one academic term (usually a semester or a summer term). Social sciences and humanities dominate the fields of study. This disparity between incoming and outbound students is one of the major challenges in internationalization efforts. Some campuses have had great success in sending as many as 40 to 90 percent of their undergraduates abroad, but barriers still limit access, particularly for graduate students, engineering students, and students with disabilities.

International student service units often interact with campus admissions offices, residence hall staff, student health and counseling centers, English language programs, and faculty advisors. Study-abroad services tend to interact with host institutions overseas, financial aid offices, academic departments, and registrars or other transfer credit evaluators, although there is a trend to work more closely with student affairs offices, particularly in the area of health and safety.

Staffing (Roles and Responsibilities)

The primary role of international student advisors (the midlevel administrators) is to assist international students in adjusting to and succeeding in obtaining degrees from U.S. institutions. This encompasses services and activities such as the following:

- Orientation for new students
- Ongoing advising throughout the year on cross-cultural issues such as adjusting to the U.S. style of higher education, understanding U.S. medical insurance and health care, dealing with family concerns (for example, spouses and children who do not speak English), and loneliness
- Providing cocurricular programs to offer professional development, leadership, and social opportunities
- Preparing students to explore postgraduation opportunities or to return home at the end of their studies
- Working with faculty, students, and staff to facilitate an understanding of cultural contexts by which international students may be operating or communicating

An increasing amount of advisors' time over the past decades has been spent in dealing with students' visa-related needs. Immigration regulations regarding international students have become much more complex and difficult to administer. In addition, government reporting requirements have increased, requiring much closer monitoring of student activities and progress. Events such as the Iran hostage crisis, the Tiananmen Square uprising, ethnic warfare in Europe and Africa, and the Asian economic crisis have often caused tremendous upheaval in the lives of students from those regions, raising concerns about the welfare of loved ones back home and whether they will be able to return home safely. At the same time, as the U.S. government responds to those situations in the context of global diplomacy, students may fear for the security of their legal status here. In these types of situations, advisors often interact with both campus and government officials to assist international students at their campuses.

Similarly, although the routine responsibilities of study-abroad advisors include predeparture orientation for students going overseas (specific cross-cultural information, support for academic advising and adjustment abroad, and reentry programs for a smooth transition back to higher education in the United States), they, too, often face intense and complex challenges such as natural disasters or political events overseas. The parents at home are invariably distraught as they see dramatic news coverage from far away and often contact the university study-abroad office for assistance. International education professionals frequently act as the go-betweens in establishing communication and ensuring that students are safe and healthy. This sometimes involves working with the U.S. Department of State or other agencies and at times may even include trips abroad to bring students home.

The international education profession tends to attract young, enthusiastic new recruits, many of whom have had a positive international experience of some sort. Many have taught English as a foreign language overseas, many have participated in study-abroad programs, some are ex–Peace Corps volunteers, and some are former international students who chose to remain in the United States. The field is made up predominantly of Caucasians and women, though ethnic minorities comprise a higher share of the field than in many administrative areas (approximately 17 percent), in part due to the numbers of international students who have stayed in the United States to become international education administrators (NAFSA: Association of International Educators, 1999). The majority of international affairs administrators have at least a master's degree.

International student services and study-abroad offices vary in size and structure depending on the institution. Some units are one-person offices, as it were, with little or no clerical support, whereas other offices have a director, assistant or associate director, several advisors, clerical staff, and student help. Offices oftentimes rely on part-time student employees, many of whom may be international students or study-abroad returnees; these student workers can be invaluable linguistic and cultural resources for professional staff, although their skills need to be used judiciously when dealing with their fellow students. International student affairs offices may also host paid or unpaid interns who want to launch careers in international education.

Among the factors that guide international student affairs administrators in following a career path are the stability of their institution and whether they choose to stay in one place or move between institutions. For instance, a newcomer to the field might work in an international living center or residence hall for a year and then take an entry-level international student advisor position and subsequently move up to become assistant director or director. Other professionals may stay in the same institution but change or add responsibilities when the campus reorganizes; such changes may include bringing international admissions or an intensive English language program under the umbrella of a larger international student affairs unit. Still other midcareer administrators may feel that they cannot advance in one institution and so move to a new campus with greater opportunities.

These career paths are substantially similar for both international student advisors and study-abroad advisors, though the latter may spend part of their careers in private sector organizations that facilitate independent study-abroad programs.

Major Functional Challenges of the Unit

As with many administrative units, one of the great challenges in international student affairs is how to respond to competing demands from multiple constituencies. International education administrators are usually drawn to the field because they enjoy interacting with people, particularly those from other cultures, so they get their greatest rewards from providing direct services to students. At the same time, professionals are required to represent the interests of their institutions and must follow campus policies and procedures, even when they may not seem to be in the best interests of their students. Finally, these professionals end up working extensively with federal regulations and agencies, ranging from the Immigration and Naturalization Service (INS), the State Department, and the Department of Education to the Internal Revenue Service. Thus, developing expertise in highly technical regulatory matters, acting as a midlevel professional in a web of institutional bureaucracy, and maintaining an appreciation for human interaction and cultural diversity all at the same time present an ongoing challenge.

Another challenge in some institutions is the marginalization of international student affairs. Unfortunately, offices that serve special populations, whether they be minority students, students with disabilities, international students, or other groups that appear to be on the periphery of the institution's mission, are sometimes treated either as fluff programs that are nice but expendable or, in bad fiscal times, as a drain on limited campus resources. Administrators in these situations should plan on devoting time and energy to raising the visibility of their offices and advocating for their function's centrality to the institutional mission and goals. In offices that are already overworked and understaffed, this additional responsibility can become wearisome but is vital if internationalization is indeed one of the institution's substantive commitments.

In addition to on-campus advocacy, international education administrators are often expected to be advocates off campus as well. It is becoming more commonplace for these midlevel professionals to share information with the campus legal affairs or government relations office to educate state and federal elected officials on issues that can help or hinder campus internationalization activities. For instance, a number of states and the federal government currently believe there is a need to crack down on perceived immigration problems; their subsequent actions are likely to hamper campus efforts to attract more international students and researchers. Midlevel international student advisors are finding that they need to become more proactive and much more politically astute in dealing with these situations.

Professional Challenges and Support Systems

Fortunately, international education administrators may turn to sources of information and support for help in dealing with the many challenges of the field. Professional associations, which are discussed in detail in the following paragraphs, can provide guidance in defining appropriate standards for international education administrators. Associations set baseline standards of performance and measures of competence that enable the individual administrator to have a framework that defines professional success.

NAFSA: The Association of International Educators (formerly the National Association for Foreign Student Affairs) is the primary professional association for midlevel administrators in all areas of international education programs, with over 8,000 members around the world. It is divided into professional sections for those who work in admissions, international student advising, study abroad, English as a second language programs, and community programming. The organization is also divided into eleven geographic regions in the United States, each with its own leadership structure, to provide more avenues for networking among colleagues.

NAFSA upholds clearly defined professional standards for international educators. It has a statement of professional competencies and a code of ethics. Because many aspects of the field cannot be learned in traditional degree programs, NAFSA provides its members with a comprehensive professional development program of structured training workshops in the various aspects of international education as well as regional and national conferences. The organization also has an active advocacy arm that assists members in working with their state and federal legislators on issues that affect international education. In addition, NAFSA maintains a job registry for those seeking to enter or change jobs in the profession.

NAFSA offers its midlevel and senior members opportunities to take leadership roles in the organizations, to provide training for others in the field, and to publish materials for member use. Such activities provide creative and professional outlets for midcareer administrators, especially those who may not have similar opportunities for advancement and recognition on their campuses.

International student services administrators may also be affiliated with one or more of the following professional associations, depending on the specific duties of their positions:

- Association of International Education Administrators (AIEA)
- Teachers of English to Speakers of Other Languages (TESOL)
- American Association of Collegiate Registrars and Admissions Officers (AACRAO)
- NASPA: Student Affairs Administrators in Higher Education (formerly the National Association of Student Personnel Administrators)

- American College Personnel Association (ACPA)
- College and University Personnel Association (CUPA)

Professional Literature

Scholarly research in the field of international student affairs is limited. Because international mobility of students is relatively easy within the European Union, some research by European educators focuses on international students and administration of international programs. Periodically, one can find articles in higher education journals, but few scholarly publications are specifically devoted to international student affairs. Some journals with an international education focus include the *Journal of International Higher Education, International Journal of Intercultural Research,* and *TESOL Quarterly,* though the scope of these publications is much broader than just international student affairs.

With regard to professional rather than scholarly publications, NAFSA publishes a journal, *International Educator,* which addresses current events and policy issues in the field. Although *International Educator* focuses more heavily on practice than on scholarship, it increasingly relies on new research to inform policy and practice discussions. Another key source of useful data for international student affairs professionals is *Open Doors,* an annual compendium of demographic data and trends in international education published by the Institute of International Education (IIE). In addition, IIE and NAFSA both publish professional papers and monographs on various topics in international student affairs. However, scholarly research conducted and published by professional associations is limited. Policy studies and program assessments based on scholarly research are greatly needed but are still a relatively new arena. Graduate students in search of thesis or dissertation topics with real-world applications will find fertile ground in international education administration.

Tips for Those Interested in the Field

Develop an appreciation for cultural and human complexity. This includes being able to view the world through multiple perspectives simultaneously. It is especially helpful to develop your skills in translating cultural contexts for others and to hone your communication skills, especially listening. Specific ways to develop these skills follow.

Engage in an international living experience. Travel, work, or study abroad. This will help you develop empathy for others who are grappling with a new culture. It will also help increase your tolerance for uncertainty and ambiguity—skills that all administrators need to survive. If you can not go outside of the country, at least engage yourself in meaningful activities in culturally different communities in your area.

Study a language. You may never actually use another language on a regular basis while working in international student services (unless your job includes travel abroad), but it will increase your empathy for other language learners who struggle to express themselves in a new idiom, both at home and abroad.

Obtain hands-on experience. Do an internship in an international student services or study-abroad unit. Start developing the technical and regulatory knowledge that pertains to your intended career, for example, visa regulations for international students in the United States or financial aid for study abroad. Get some experience in mediation or conflict resolution through a community organization.

Get an advanced degree. Help advance the profession by conducting sound scholarly research and sharing it with others in the field. Some popular fields of scholarship are area studies, intercultural studies, educational administration, and college-student personnel, though many fields have relevance to the profession.

Career Paths of the Authors

Author 1: Melinda Wood. I had my first taste of international adventure when my father, who was in the U.S. military, was assigned overseas. I attended a U.S. Department of Defense high school in Okinawa, which at the time was a U.S. protectorate and now is the southernmost prefecture of Japan. I was there during a time of great political turmoil—the Vietnam War, right before Okinawa reverted to the Japanese government. Toward the end of my senior year of high school, armed marines accompanied our school buses from one military base to the next to protect us from angry demonstrators who did not want their small island drawn further into U.S. geopolitical aspirations abroad. At the same time, my family, like many military families in Okinawa, had a number of Okinawan friends, and we enjoyed getting involved in life off the military base. Thus, I was acutely aware of the divergent roles one plays as an individual and as a representative (willing or not) of one's nation.

During my university years I realized that I wanted to live abroad again, so I obtained a master's degree in teaching English as a foreign language. A Japanese classmate helped me to find a teaching job in Japan, where I stayed for nearly three years. I lived in a city that had relatively few foreigners, so I became used to being a minority and a novelty. The greatest shock of that experience was returning to the United States and finding that my reverse culture shock, as it is sometimes called, was far more intense than the process of adjusting to Japan. I continued to teach English to immigrants, refugees, and pre-university foreign students to maintain my involvement with people from other countries and cultures.

Later I worked with a homestay program, placing international students in U.S. families' homes. Then I got my first job as a university foreign student advisor, combining my previous experiences in teaching, service, and administration. Little did I realize that the institution was in economic crisis and in danger of closing its doors in the near future. Fortunately, I worked for a director who was both creative and astute, which allowed her to parlay the crisis into an opportunity to reorganize. The international education office was merged with several others, and I became a more generalized student services administrator. Most of my duties were still with international students, but I was better able to learn how student services form an integrated unit.

My next career move was to become associate director of a student services unit in a different institution that was comprised of almost equal numbers of domestic students and international students. Subsequently, I became director of the office. Thus, in about ten years I had risen from entry-level international student advisor to director of a student services unit. There had been a few lateral moves and title changes and one move to a new institution, but basically I had covered nearly the full spectrum of the administrative ladder in one decade. Subsequently, the entire office was downsized in a budget crisis, and its duties were dispersed through other administrative units. Perhaps in larger institutions there would be alternatives within the bureaucracy to which one could move or advance, but not in my personal experience.

Since leaving that position, I have been working in a number of short-term university jobs using my international education background while completing my doctorate in higher education administration. My intention is to return to full-time employment in university administration, perhaps in international education or another area where my international background will be an additional asset.

Author 2: Parandeh Kia. My first venture overseas was my trip from Iran to the United States for the last year of high school, at the tail end of what was the largest influx of Iranian students to the U.S. I spent a year in a high school in Iowa's corn belt, where I learned a great deal about the language and culture of the country, far removed from the cosmopolitan life of the two coasts. Along with a high school exchange student in my class, I was one of the two foreigners in town. Our presence was embraced with warmth and great generosity as we engrossed ourselves in the life of our rural surroundings, religiously attending Friday night football and basketball games, paying close attention to farm news, and answering naive questions about what our respective countries were like.

After that first year of learning about the United States, the tide turned when I entered college and Iran was in the grip of an Islamic revolution. The events of the following few years greatly altered the life of many Iranians living in the United States. Along with thousands of my peers, I recall showing up dutifully at the INS district office in Omaha with all my papers intact, reporting in, like the good farm girl I'd learned to be, long before I understood why and how that process was considered unconstitutional. I continued in college, thanks to the grace of and emotional support from many people, while I earned a living at various jobs, ultimately finding myself in a student worker position on campus at the international center. I stayed in school because there was really nothing else that I could do—being an Iranian in the United States continued to be a liability in the aftermath of the hostage crisis.

I started my professional career in an entry-level advising job working with international students. Because of my interest and success in programming, I was promoted to assistant director. After a few years, it became clear that even though in my role as an international student advisor I had often crossed into and succeeded in other areas of student affairs such as residence life, student activities, and career advising, my institution would always see me as working with international students—which clearly was not valued as highly within student affairs. There was to be no opportunity for professional growth unless my supervisor in the international office left or I moved on.

I moved to a small college as a director to set up an office working with international students. I believed I had located an opportunity for developing an international office that included international students as well as Americans going abroad. I came to realize that faculty involvement in study abroad was offered as a token preretirement junket for a faculty member with long, close ties to the administration. There would not be much room to develop programs for international students as the numbers were small and commitment seemed lacking. Thus, I chose to move to a new position at a large state school that combined study abroad and services for international students and scholars. I worked in the latter area with major responsibility for immigration and advising of scholars.

My next move was to a major research institution that had enjoyed a large international student population for years but provided no major services or support for this group. I had a chance to develop a program and was soon promoted to a directorial position, which I currently hold. In subsequent years, in part because a large number of our graduate students are international students and in response to the growing commitment of the institution to improving the quality of student life, a new position as an associate dean in the graduate school was created, and I was promoted to fill that position while continuing to direct the services for international students.

References

Davis, Todd. *Open Doors 1998–99.* New York: Institute of International Education, 1999.

NAFSA: Association of International Educators. "The Way We See It." Report of the 1998–99 NAFSA Membership Survey. [http://www.nafsa.org]. 1999.

NAFSA: Association of International Educators. "International Education Factsheet." [http://www.nafsa.org]. 2000.

MELINDA WOOD *is assistant to the chancellor at the University of Hawai'i–West Oahu.*

PARANDEH KIA *is associate dean of the graduate school and director of international student services at California Technical School.*

7

Enrollment management as an organizational model has become a positive foundation for the strengthening of an institution's enrollment by integrating seven primary functional areas.

Enrollment Management

Thomas Huddleston Jr.

"The radical underlying commitment of enrollment management is its unswerving focus on the longitudinal care and comprehensive education of students" (Keller, 1991, p. 3). This statement captures the essence of enrollment management in focusing on the long-term welfare of the student and the entirety of the collegiate experience.

The first book about enrollment management, published in 1982, defined the program as an assertive approach to ensuring the steady supply of qualified students required to maintain institutional vitality (Kemerer, Baldridge, and Green, 1982). Other authors have voiced broader definitions. For example, Michael G. Dolence (1993, p. 8) defines enrollment management as "[a] comprehensive process designed to help an institution achieve and maintain the optimum recruitment, retention and graduation rates of students . . . [a]n institution-wide process that embraces virtually every aspect of an institution's function and culture."

Optimally, an institution's enrollment is comprehensively developed and is based on a strategic, integrative plan that includes the identification, attraction, selection, encouragement, registration, retention, and graduation of targeted student segments. The quality of the students' collegiate experience is based largely on the academic environment, operational excellence of the institution's transition programs, student services, and personal development opportunities. Within this broad context, an enrollment manager's efforts are intended to shape and influence particular units that have significant impact on a student's decision to enroll, persist, and graduate. The strategic management of these units is important to an institution's growth, fiscal health, and student satisfaction.

Enrollment management may be structured within the administration as a formal committee, implemented through a matrix structure, or managed as a comprehensive enrollment division. Integration, communication, and collaboration with the academic affairs area are critical for a model's successful operation, long-term viability, and acceptance by the campus community (Huddleston, 1999).

Background

Enrollment management, as a concept and process, remains relatively new to higher education. Developed initially within private institutions, the enrollment management concept soon spread to public institutions and gained popularity among two-year colleges.

The development of enrollment management occurred in response to a widespread focus on increasing new student enrollments. Concern for larger and more profitable enrollments in private colleges served as the impetus to develop an operational unit that would increase the integration, efficiency, and effectiveness of key operations; improve tactics and strategies of those areas to strengthen articulation with prospective students; and following enrollment, enhance the retention of those new students. These new directions became the springboard for new thinking and organizational change that would build enrollment demand and provide more focus on the students' collegiate experience.

In a national study conducted by Huddleston and Rumbough (1997), seven functional areas were most frequently identified as enrollment management units by colleges and universities: institutional research and planning, marketing, admissions, registrar, financial aid, student orientation, and retention and advising. Each of these functional areas plays a key role within an enrollment model that strengthens the opportunities for institutional success. The shared missions, primary goals, and the integration and interdependence of these key areas are vital to the successful implementation and operation of enrollment management.

Institutional Research and Planning

Focused planning and research are one of the first steps in the enrollment management process (Hossler, 1996). An integrated research and planning effort can enable colleges and universities to remain sensitive to the marketplace and carefully assess external social trends and internal strengths and weaknesses, relative to the attraction of new students, and their retention and graduation at the university. Research and planning inform the strategic directions of enrollment managers. An institutional research effort manages and provides relevant data including retention rates, historical trends, registration statistics, student characteristics, and enrollment patterns and projections.

Such data can frame the enrollment needs and objectives and identify relevant issues for additional discussion. For example, discovering what prospective and current students perceive to be important as well as the corresponding level of satisfaction is essential. Additionally, salient questions pertaining to information needs and the communication of findings to the campus community are integral to research and planning within the enrollment management arena (see Chapters Eight and Eleven for further discussion of these functions).

Marketing

The application of marketing principles and strategies has become commonplace within colleges and universities, particularly within admissions offices. Employing marketing concepts, educational institutions have formulated plans that create institutional awareness, identify student demographics, project student demand, and develop enrollment and retention plans. The comprehensive value of marketing is reflected in Krachenberg's classic definition: "Marketing deals with the concept of uncovering specific needs, satisfying these needs by the development of appropriate goods and services, letting people know of their availability, and offering them at appropriate prices, at the right time and place" (1972, p. 380). This early definition served as a basis for the implementation of increased marketing within higher education.

To understand the marketplace, each enrollment organization should obtain data concerning students who apply, matriculate, persist, and graduate. The data collected serve as a springboard for the employment of strategic marketing plans, most typically coordinated by the admissions office.

Admissions

Today's admissions office is responsible for numerous functions, all of which must take place within an environment of rising tuition costs, the special interests and needs of the institution, and the competitive marketplace for students. In today's environment, the admissions office is expected to produce significant revenues based on student headcount, while concomitantly being asked to focus on quality and other student characteristics. Within their objectives for admissions, institutions balance desired revenue, student quality, diversity, campus resources, selectivity, service to the community, and maintenance of academic majors (G. D. Chavis Jr., executive director of undergraduate admissions at the University of Central Florida, personal communication, Jan. 2000).

The admissions office is responsible for a variety of activities including generating interest in the institution by creating a comprehensive student profile, identifying and contacting the potential pool, converting prospective students into applicants, maintaining consistent contact with the applicants to sustain their interest in the institution, coordinating programs and activities to help sustain that interest through the application process, hosting yield enhancement activities to encourage enrollment, providing quality customer service, and maintaining and developing constituent relations with various community leaders.

Janet Lavin Rapelye's summary statement about admissions professionals suggests the importance of their work: "As admission professionals, we are simultaneously educators and business managers, bringing in millions of dollars of revenue to our institutions and (hopefully) spending smaller amounts in financial aid. We serve as advisors to our presidents, spokespeople to our alumni/ae and the outside world including the media, leaders to our staffs, and, if we are fortunate, counselors to our college students. We deliver the class to the faculty, calculate the statistics for our trustees, fill out questionnaire after questionnaire for guidebooks and survey groups, and work with parents, guidance counselors and students" (1999, p. 23).

Registrar

Historically, a close synergy has existed between the registrar and the admissions office. Functions such as admissions processing were once housed in the registrar's area. As institutions grew, separate admissions offices emerged to provide more attention to new enrollment growth.

Relevant to any enrollment management model, the office of the registrar manages the registration of students, student records, class schedules, catalogue production, classroom utilization, academic calendar, centralized information systems, and policy and procedural practices in accordance with state and federal guidelines. The office's professional staff are typically involved in the development and management of technological innovations within the campus community. Personnel are required to supervise and utilize management information systems for reports and programs of the academic infrastructure.

Cooperation between admissions and registrar offices are now commonplace. Today, the American Association of College Registrars and Admissions Officers (AACRAO) has extended its influence to include the national sponsorship of Strategic Enrollment Management (SEM) seminars and publications.

Financial Aid

The importance of financial assistance continues to loom large for colleges and their students. Enrollment management personnel are aware of the importance that financial assistance has on college choice. Family lifestyle, socioeconomic status, or social educational values may preclude or encourage the decision to attend a particular college. Colleges can affect the perceived value of their product through their tuition pricing and financial aid strategies. Financial aid administrators are crucial to enrollment planning both for the support of new student enrollments and for student retention.

The financial aid office responds to student and family questions and concerns regarding financial aid availability and distribution including packaging of state and federal monies, grants, loans, and scholarships; institutional aid; need-based and merit-based assistance; and expected family contributions. The financial aid office also remains responsive to institutional needs, particularly those related to enrollments and revenues while ensuring compliance with federal and state regulations.

Student Orientation

Perigo and Upcraft (1989, p. 82) define the orientation program as "any effort to help freshmen make the transition from their previous environment to the collegiate environment and enhance their success." The role of the orientation process within the enrollment management framework is to strengthen student transition and retention. Orientation may be the first confirmation of the image that has been conveyed by a college. A typical orientation program will aid students in their academic success by providing information about advisement, registration, housing, the administration of placement tests, cocurricular activities, and the transition to college life.

The orientation process should provide students and their families with realistic expectations of college life at that institution. Also, the orientation process provides an opportunity for the institution to learn about the student (Perigo and Upcraft, 1989). Although most orientation periods are a few days in length, the process is essential for building affiliation and appreciation of educational opportunities at that institution. Extended orientation programs for one semester or longer are gaining popularity and seem to enhance the potential for student success.

Retention and Advising

Student retention is a widespread concern among colleges and universities. At least 40 percent of all entering students will not complete a baccalaureate degree in the college where they initially enroll within five years (National Center for Education Statistics, 1996). A successful retention program, as part of an enrollment management effort, has broad benefits, including fiscal stability for the institution (Peterson, 1991).

A campus retention program is based on appropriate research among selected student groups. Examples of needed data include student persistence rates, course success rates, nonresidence statistics, and selection of academic majors. Targeted studies can be designed to examine student relationships with the college and identify attrition-prone students. Findings from these studies provide information about why students leave or remain at the institution. These data can assist in directing the efforts of an institutional retention audit and plan. Dennis (1998) acknowledges the difficulty of implementing practical and effective retention management practices. She notes the need for involving a wide variety of campus personnel and generating campus-wide support.

Student retention outcomes are considered by some educators to be key performance indicators of a successful collegiate experience. From a student perspective, educational and vocational advising are vital to their persistence in college. Effective academic and career advisement programs are paramount in retaining students at all levels within an educational setting (see Chapter Two for a more thorough discussion of advising).

Trends

Enrollment management models have been adopted on numerous campuses (Huddleston and Rumbough, 1997). They differ in scope and influence depending on institutional goals, revenue requirements, internal culture, and the competitive marketplace. Within public institutions, most enrollment management organizations report to a provost or vice president of academic affairs. In private institutions, enrollment managers are more likely to report directly to the president.

Both public and private institutions indicate that interest in increasing enrollment is the main reason for changing to an enrollment management structure. Intended benefits include increased enrollment, improved efficiency of the units within an enrollment model, expanded marketing capabilities, enhanced quality of new students, and stronger internal and external communication of student information.

The implementation of successful retention strategies remains a challenge, however, for enrollment management specialists at most colleges and universities. Retention crosses many fundamental areas of an institution. Most institutions have not designated a professional charged to coordinate and take responsibility for successful outcomes; rather, most rely on a campus-wide retention committee.

Examining demographics; improving access; linking pricing, aid, and institutional budgets; achieving student diversity; attracting and serving international and adult students; developing campus retention programs; managing information systems; using integrated communication; creating a marketing plan; enhancing student services; establishing predictive modeling; measuring the success of academic support programs; and establishing desired program outcomes and assessment measures represent some of the important issues that are being addressed by enrollment management teams, institutes, and conferences.

Careers in Enrollment Management

As can be seen by the variety of functional areas described, many potential opportunities exist for individuals desiring employment within an enrollment management arena. Because of the diversity of offices that compose the enrollment management system, employment opportunities may be found nationwide at a variety of postsecondary educational institutions.

Historically, most enrollment management practitioners have had a background in college admissions. Other practitioners have built their careers in financial aid, the registration office, institutional research, and student affairs. Regardless of functional background, the successful director of a comprehensive enrollment management program must possess many attributes. Previous administrative management of a primary area in the enrollment management area, creativity, leadership, task orientation, understanding of fundamental marketing concepts, interpersonal skills, team management experience, and familiarity with higher education are essential components for a successful enrollment professional. A master's degree or doctorate is a common educational credential.

Professional organizations assist in the generation, compilation, and dissemination of information of pertaining to specific fundamental areas. They also provide a forum for networking and exploration of career opportunities (see Appendix for a list of the professional associations relevant to enrollment management).

Private vendors that provide collegiate publications, information systems, and general marketing services also play key roles in strengthening knowledge about enrollment management strategies. Additionally, publications including newsletters, articles, and books discussing enrollment management are available. A recent sign of the increased professionalization of the field is the creation of a master's degree program at the University of Miami in enrollment management ("UM Offers First Graduate Program . . . ," 1998).

Conclusion

The concepts and practices implemented within an enrollment management model have improved student services and learning. Today, we know that enrollment should be comprehensive in focus and requires greater attention than a singular admissions office. The success of the enrollment management idea has been the identification and integration of key administrative units that work together to strengthen the student's chance for academic success and the institution's competitive advantage.

The environment in which enrollment managers work has changed from college recruiters targeting traditional markets to a larger focus that requires broader management skills and knowledge base. Today, attention is also required to nontraditional students, community colleges, graduate programs, and branch campuses. New technology, on-line services, distance education learning programs, for-profit competitors, and student services must be considered.

Enrollment management provides a positive career option for professionals in higher education. The future will continue to bring new enrollment challenges that colleges and universities must address to remain viable. Enrollment management principles and practices continue to offer a comprehensive means to address these challenges.

Career Profile: Thomas Huddleston Jr.

After earning an undergraduate and master's degree at Texas A&M, Huddleston began his professional career in corporate public relations and association management before being asked to return to his alma mater to develop that institution's first admissions office. He later earned his doctorate in education and taught while serving as assistant to the head of the School of Journalism at Oklahoma State University. In the fall of 1971, Huddleston accepted the position of dean of admissions at Bentley College in Waltham, Massachusetts. He continued to increase his knowledge about strategic marketing applications for the nonprofit sector and worked closely with the New England College Board, the New England Association College Admissions Counselors, and the New England Association of Collegiate Registrars and Admissions Officers.

Huddleston moved to Bradley University as dean of admissions and financial aid. During his nine years at the university, he advanced from his initial position to assistant vice president of student life planning and, later, associate provost for student affairs. During this time, Huddleston led collegiate marketing institutes, published numerous articles on the use of marketing strategies, consulted, and initiated geodemography strategies to strengthen Bradley's enrollment opportunities.

He left Bradley to become the director of worldwide marketing for Sperry Corporation's education industry segment and, later, the head of student financial systems at National Computer Systems. He continued to serve as an educational consultant and eventually elected to remain at one of his assignments, Spring Hill College, as the vice president for institutional advancement. Responsible for various enrollment and student service functions, he also joined the College Board's Summer Institute and helped develop the institute's enrollment management track. Later he accepted a position at Saint Joseph's University in Philadelphia as associate vice president for enrollment.

From there, Huddleston joined the University of Central Florida in Orlando, where he now serves as vice president for student development and enrollment services. He continues to speak at various forums, remains active with professional associations, and is the co-director of the College Board's Summer Institute on College Admissions.

References

Dennis, M. J. *A Practical Guide to Enrollment and Retention Management in Higher Education.* Westport, Conn.: Bergin & Garvey, 1998.

Dolence, M. G. *Strategic Enrollment Management: A Primer for Campus Administrators.* Washington, D.C.: American Association of Collegiate Registrars and Admissions Officers, 1993.

Hossler, D. "From Admissions to Enrollment Management." In A. L. Rentz (ed.), *Student Affairs Practice in Higher Education.* (2nd ed.) Springfield, Ill.: Charles C. Thomas, 1996.

Huddleston, T., Jr. "Developing the Enrollment Model at Four-Year Institutions." Paper presented at The College Board Seminar, Atlanta, Georgia, May 1999.

Huddleston, T., Jr., and Rumbough, L. P. "Evaluating the Enrollment Management Organization." *College and University,* 1997, 72(4), 2–5.

Keller, G. "Introduction: The Role of Student Affairs in Institution-Wide Enrollment Management Strategies." In A. Galsky (ed.), *The Role of Student Affairs in Institution-Wide Enrollment Management Strategies.* Washington, D.C.: The National Association of Student Personnel Administrators, 1991.

Kemerer, F., Baldridge, J. V., and Green, K. *Strategies for Effective Enrollment Management.* Washington, D.C.: American Association of State Colleges and Universities, 1982.

Krachenberg, A. R. "Bringing the Concept of Marketing to Higher Education." *Journal of Higher Education,* 1972, 43(5), 369–380.

National Center for Education Statistics. "Indicator 10." *The Condition of Education 1996,* 212.

Perigo, D. J., and Upcraft, M. L. "Orientation Programs." In M. L. Upcraft and J. N. Gardner (eds.), *The Freshman Year Experience: Helping Students Survive and Succeed in College.* San Francisco: Jossey-Bass, 1989.

Peterson, M. W. *Organization and Governance in Higher Education.* (4th ed.) Needham Heights, Mass.: Simon & Schuster, 1991.

Rapelye, J. L. "Who Are We Now?" *The Journal of College Admission,* 1999, 163 (Spring-Summer), 22–29.

"UM Offers First Graduate Program in Enrollment Management in U.S." University of Miami NEWS [http://www.miami.edu/visitors/news/releases/]. July 9, 1998.

THOMAS HUDDLESTON JR. is vice president for student development and enrollment services at the University of Central Florida.

8

A close integration of university-level planning and budget is required to drive change.

Budget and Planning

Patricia N. Haeuser

Every institution of higher education engages in planning and developing a budget, but it is perhaps more luck than common occurrence that these functions are combined into a single office. Even if not formally aligned, however, individuals with responsibility for university-level planning and budget know that a close integration is required to drive change. Starting with this critical linkage is important because it exemplifies a key concern of midlevel administrators: effectively harnessing the tools and politics that surround their areas of responsibility and interest.

Budget and Planning: "So happy together . . ."

A planning office is one of those areas in higher education whose home (or homes, as there is strategic planning, long-range planning, academic planning, budget planning, capital planning, and so on), roles, and responsibilities vary widely. A vast planning literature by Keller (1983); Hardy, Langley, Mintzberg, and Rose (1983); Norris and Poulton (1991); Norris and Morrison (1997), and many others discusses types of planning and provides advice about key ingredients for improving planning efforts. One of the important factors in effective planning is developing a method to align resources with plans. It also helps to consider that budgeting is a "a process of *making decisions that distribute resources to enable action.* . . . First, the definition calls attention to the obvious but often overlooked fact that a budget represents a collection of decisions. . . . Second, the definition serves to reinforce the notion that the purpose of the budget is to implement the institution's plans; the budget is a major (but not the only) tool for ensuring that institutional goals are pursued and, in the end, achieved" (Vandement and Jones, 1993, p. 5).

NEW DIRECTIONS FOR HIGHER EDUCATION, no. 111, Fall 2000 © Jossey-Bass, a Wiley company

Linking planning and budgeting gains even greater power with good leadership and a participatory approach that involves faculty and staff in strategic decision making (McLagan and Nel, 1995; Ziegler, 1999). Of course, as well as the combination of leadership, planning, budget, and participation, the literature points out many other factors important for effective performance—for example, environmental impacts, interpersonal relationships, quality of information, timeliness, and so on. Nevertheless, for planners and budgeters the combination of leadership support, planning, budget, and a participatory process usually provides the capability to affect an institution's performance at some level.

Effective Change and Planning and Budget Offices: The Holy Grail

"Above all, we need to acknowledge that strategic change is closer to theater than to science, closer to tragedy than to carving soap" (Keller, 1998, p. 23). The higher education literature vividly portrays the challenges of a planning position (Mintzberg, 1994; Norris and Poulton, 1991; Harvey, 1998; Schmidtlein and Milton, 1989, 1990), and the Society for College and University Planning (SCUP) publishes several articles an issue in its journal *Planning for Higher Education* that describe difficulties and prescriptive solutions associated with various types of planning. Planners face issues such as lack of real support from leadership, planning processes that ignore the external environment or have little relevance to actual institutional actions, problems with top-down and bottom-up communication, an institutional lack of focus and purpose, insufficient attention being paid to the effects of plans, and so on. As Schmidtlein and Milton (1989) have found, many planning efforts or processes are abandoned or refashioned within three years of their initiation.

Many similar concerns are voiced in the literature on effective budget principles and practices. The American Productivity and Quality Center has conducted a project (1996) to examine best practices in higher education budgeting and identified the following budget goals:

1. Use the institutional budgeting process to help focus and achieve the institution's overall strategic goals.
2. Improve budget practices through linking of strategy, mission and budget, and effective use of internal and external data.
3. Support and create an institutional budgeting process that is efficient, uses incentives and reallocation strategies, and considers the needs of affected constituencies while meeting the needs of the institution (pp. 1–6).

Strategic budgeting is a term that signifies hoped-for strong linkages between planning and budgeting; it is elusive as a reality, however, as institutional and external forces conspire against it. Sell and Moen (1998, p. 1) point to good planning, which they refer to as *just-in-time planning*, as requiring two dimensions: time horizons (flexible plans within strategic boundaries that are readjusted as external environmental changes demand) and "spaciousness" of involvement (that is, including all relevant campus actors). Burke has studied whether campuses' budgeting practices followed the essential principles of collaborative planning, longer-term as well as short-term plans and strategies, and fundamental change, and he concludes that "the overall record of institutional practices compared with budget principles proved disappointing, though perhaps not surprising" (1998, p. 25).

Too often, however, the typical budget practices found in higher education reflect apathy of least resistance, that is, a path that provides leaders with control and faculty and staff with few surprises or changes. Hierarchical decision making, incremental or formula budgeting, across-the-board reduction, avoidance of mission shaping, and withholding of information can be very efficient budget-shaping strategies. At its worse, such strategies can lead to campus budget processes (and, as a result, budgets) that are mysterious and opaque to most faculty and staff. When done well, with sensitivity to campus culture, this type of process may be successful for years and years—until a key senior administrative leader leaves or retires, a budget shortfall intervenes, and so on. When not administered adroitly, the closed budget process often becomes a focal point for dissatisfaction.

Major Professional Challenges: Tilting at Windmills

These functional challenges have direct implications as professional challenges for budget and planning administrators. In a playful way, Keller (1998, p. 18) reminds planners that they need to understand human nature—whether their audience be Freudian, Marxist, or Darwinian in orientation—to effect change. Norris and Poulton (1991, p. 6) more formally suggest that successful planners should be practical and insightful about the organization, understanding the role of different stakeholders in the outcomes of planning. It would be foolish to disagree with this good advice, but possessing and regularly manifesting insight, understanding, and political savvy is a challenge for anyone and is perhaps an even bigger challenge for the midlevel administrator.

As an administrator in the middle, the manager often must simultaneously push senior leaders to identify strategies to lead the institution and then pull them back from moving too quickly to implement their ideas. There is almost always some tension between encouraging participation and openness in budget and planning processes and a leader's desire or need to show that he or she is effective and decisive. Similarly, friction exists between being sensitive to how and why people will react to ideas and the need to move past legitimate yet parochial concerns so that farsighted decisions can be made.

Adherence to good principles would require these administrators to take risks, but institutional budgetary change ruffles feathers almost as much as salary, benefit, and parking changes. The administrator in the middle may be blamed if senior-level administrators withdraw support from the process or the faculty and staff perceive that they are being left out or ignored. As in any job, humor, honesty, integrity, and accessibility help build relationships that transcend disagreements over issues and processes.

On a practical level, people in this position usually require skills in facilitating large and small groups and in orchestrating group learning. They are required to summarize and present complex data. These midlevel administrators require the skills to chair committees as well as the ability to recruit, shape, and support faculty as effective committee chairs themselves. This latter point may be somewhat sensitive but is pertinent to serving an intermediary function in a higher education environment.

Quite frequently, faculty operating either in defense of faculty rights and responsibilities or from an inflated sense of their role's importance—or both—will be somewhat dismissive of the expertise or responsibilities of midlevel administrators who did not originate from the faculty. Usually this chafing over roles is easily overcome with familiarity and evidence of fair dealing. Even in smooth times, however, the midlevel administrator may choose to work with a faculty chair to benefit from the credibility that faculty typically extend to each other.

Budget planners need to be able to develop concepts and presentations that tell a budget or planning story for the institution or for the external budget-granting agency. Keeping current with higher education issues at the national, state and local levels is essential for positioning the institution's budget plans, as does knowing when an issue is salient or likely to resonate with public officials. Every new budget planner will probably need his or her own experience to "fully swallow the toad" that all the good reasons in the world will usually not be enough to obtain additional funding. Rather, administrators get ideas funded by being able to read the environment, being attuned to the stakeholders, and understanding the institution's core needs and future directions.

Within their institutions, budget planners must know how to strategize so as to elicit action. What are the hot-button issues that need to be solved, what actions should be stimulated or discouraged, and what budget tools are available to shape behavior? Budget planners must develop a thorough understanding of budget concepts and strategies.

Finally, the challenges that budget and planning administrators face are probably very similar to those faced by other midlevel administrators. For example, most of them have been promoted from being a worker to being a manager, and the skills that a worker needs to succeed are not the skills necessary for effective management. Those managing a staff anywhere in higher education will encounter similar problems. For example, a new manager often inherits staff (who perhaps had previously been on an equivalent footing), and inherited staff typically are more challenging to motivate or develop into a team than new hires. Anywhere in education, a manager must be willing to embrace and perhaps lead in the acquisition and use of technology. The requirement to combine people and political skills with content or technique is common in higher education career building.

An Office of Budget and Planning: The Infrastructure

An interesting but simplistic research question might examine whether offices called *Budget Planning* more explicitly tie an operating budget to university plans than offices with title that includes just the word *Budget.*On the other hand, the office's title is probably less significant than its mission.

For example, as a part of a wave of significant change, the university where I am currently employed designed an open, participatory budget process. Budget, planning, and institutional research functions were combined with the following goals:

- To promote effective and efficient use of university resources through planning, analysis, alignment of resources to plan, and accountability of use
- To provide information that supports institutional planning, policy formation, and decision making
- To provide data in an independent, objective, timely, and informative manner
- To promote discussion and understanding on critical budget and planning issues leading to informed decision making

This type of mission directs and focuses energy toward the goal of linking planning and budget.

The university also organized its human resources to support the new planning and budget process. Of course, staffing of offices such as this varies with the size of the organization. In my office, as is often the case, there are three levels of staff: clerical or specialist-level assistants; mid- to senior-level analysts; and midlevel administrators, which may include assistant or associate directors as well as the director.

Clerical, assistant, or specialist positions are filled by individuals, with or without a degree, who have experience or are expected to master the operations associated with a business, accounting, or research area. The mobility of specialists is often limited to progression within the subject area for which they have gained expertise. With additional education or excellent performance, however, these individuals may gain promotion to analyst or administrative positions.

Staff members with titles such as budget and policy analyst, research analyst, policy and planning analyst, and so forth review, monitor, and evaluate policies, programs, and management practices as a guide to decision making. They design and develop studies, analytic methods, procedures, and strategies to prepare policy papers outlining alternatives and recommendations regarding a wide variety of organizational, academic, and fiscal issues. For example, studies on which my office has worked in the last year involved analyzing the fiscal implications of proposed wage increases; evaluating the likelihood of gender, ethnic, or age bias in salaries; assessing the effects of proposed individual equity adjustments; appraising peer comparisons of expenditures for specific activities; and identifying student outcomes associated with entry as an undecided student versus entry with a declared major.

Analysts typically have a master's degree and may also have a terminal degree. Their backgrounds are varied, ranging from social science to computer science and from the humanities to business. Offices that are responsible for the operating or capital budget may require an accounting or fund accounting background. Entry-level analysts are expected to possess analytic, writing, and computer skills. As in most higher education administrative positions, it helps to possess good interpersonal, teamwork, problem-solving, and organizing skills as well as creativity, enthusiasm, and the ability to meet deadlines. Good analysts are extremely valuable and have excellent mobility. Career paths might include moving into a senior analyst position, expanding analytic expertise to several areas, and being promoted to a midlevel administrative position.

Midlevel administrators (assistants, associates, and directors) distinguish themselves from analysts by their experience, expertise, education, and especially political instinct. Budget and planning midlevel administrators almost always need to present the work of their offices, involve faculty and staff in participatory and budget-building processes, and chair committees that engage in participatory decision making about the institution's resource allocations.

Promotion to midlevel budget and planning positions often results from a reputation gained within an institution or through professional associations or collaborative organizations. But equally important are unrelated happenings in the institution or external environment. Precipitating conditions such as state budget cuts or tuition revenue losses, a new change-oriented campus chief executive, a campus crisis, retirements and resignations, or changes imposed by oversight agencies as well as state or federal agencies can mean promotion or reorganization and promotion.

Professional Pathways: Highways and Byways

Budget and planning administrators may belong to the Society for College and University Planning (SCUP), the National Association of College and University Business Officers (NACUBO), the Association for Institutional Research (AIR), and state or regional affiliated organizations, all of which provide excellent training, networking, and socialization for individuals interested in budget and planning positions. Involvement in state or regional organizations provides outstanding, low-cost networking opportunities. The professional journals, newsletter, and e-mail updates and listservs sponsored or associated with these organizations are another great source of tips, contacts, and easy-entry activities.

Budget and Planning: Gazing into the Future

The longevity of budget and planning midlevel administrators may be an enlightening research topic. Because budget and planning are integral to an institution's effectiveness, the midlevel administrators in these areas may face more volatility or instability in their position than they would in some other areas in higher education. Conversely, how long do midlevel administrators elect to stay at an institution or in this position? How many are promoted to chief administrator officer, and what characteristics lead to promotion?

The theme of this chapter, that certain combinations of planning and budget are critical to effective change, provides another intriguing, if difficult, research topic. What instances of effective change falsify the claim? How does the organizational life cycle interact with the planning and budget process that an institution uses at any given time? Or how highly correlated is the planning and budget process with a president's personal leadership style?

If it is critical for higher education institutions to be able to change effectively within the context of external environmental demands and emerging trends, then higher education needs more research on the primary minimum set of concepts or variables that engender institutional success. The Malcolm Baldrige National Quality Award[1] criteria are cited as a steady and proven course for institutions to pursue excellence and success. It would be interesting to study how Baldrige organizations adapt and change over time and how their planning and budget processes (and midlevel administrators) evolve.

Director of Budget, Planning, and Analysis: My Story

Directing budget and planning for a comprehensive university was certainly not in my mind when I returned to college after spending several years as an instructor for the learning disabled. Interested in policymaking, I earned a doctorate in political science with a strong background in statistics and research methods. Like many of my colleagues with degrees in economics, sociology, psychology, and higher education, I was not willing or able to consider a career as a faculty member or part-time instructor. And like many of my colleagues, I began my entry-level position totally ignorant of the position's content.

I entered higher education as a research assistant, reporting to a registrar, and confidence that I could conduct research, write, and present on any topic led to my hiring. Then as now, an enthusiasm for computer technology and a willingness to learn new combinations of hardware and software was important. Prior to my current position, I had held six positions at two institutions.

Although I started as a research assistant, thanks to the socialization provided by a statewide research group, within six months I requested promotion to become a coordinator of institutional research. Later, when I was able to add staff, I became a director of institutional research. Although it is probably common knowledge to most, I had to learn the hard way that being promoted to a directorial level without staff to direct is very difficult; my best arguments about directing a function did not sway anyone's opinion. Then, as I assumed responsibility for planning, I became a senior director of planning and research. Finally, I added operating and capital budget planning to my duties with my last promotion.

This job progression appears smoother than it was in reality, because during this time I also moved from a public community college to a public comprehensive university. Working at different types of institutions is a terrific way to expand one's grasp of and perspective on higher education policy issues.

Sometimes it is difficult to expand from planning and research into budgeting, especially in the absence of a significant financial background. It is more common to find planners and researchers expanding into assessment, enrollment, research, grant promotion, or information technology–oriented positions. However, throughout my experience in planning and institutional research, I was watchful of opportunities to expand my responsibilities into budgeting because I believed that combination of responsibilities provided me a better chance of affecting policy and institutional change than I would encounter if I assumed other, more accessible responsibilities.

In each institution, I entered in one position and added responsibilities to it over time. I was rather lucky to be employed by an institution that was reorganizing in such a way that it made sense to integrate budget, planning, and research. It is perhaps more common that a budget officer who demonstrates political and people skills will expand into the planning role, often by promotion to higher-level administrative positions.

Note

1. The Baldrige National Quality Program is sponsored by the U.S. Department of Commerce, the National Institute of Standards and Technology, and the American Society for Quality. Last year (1999) was the first year they distributed the Baldrige Criteria for Performance Excellence in education. The Malcolm Baldrige National Quality Award is presented annually to U.S. organizations exhibiting performance excellence.

References

American Productivity and Quality Center. APQC Benchmarking Pilot Project, "Institutional Budgeting Final Report." American Productivity and Quality Center's Institute for Education Best Practices and The Pew Higher Education Roundtable, 1996.
Burke, J. C. *Managing Campus Budgets in Trying Times: Did Practices Follow Principles?* Albany, N. Y.: The Nelson Rockefeller Institute of Government, 1998.
Hardy, C., Langley, A., Mintzberg, H., and Rose, J. "Strategy Formation in the University Setting." *Review of Higher Education*, 1983, 6(4) (Summer), 407–433.

Harvey, B. C. "The Perils of Planning Before You Are Ready." *Planning for Higher Education,* 1998, 26(4), 1–9.

Keller, G. *Academic Strategy: The Management Revolution in American Higher Education.* Baltimore: The Johns Hopkins University Press, 1983.

Keller, G. "Planning, Decisions, and Human Nature." *Planning for Higher Education,* 1998, 26(2), 18–23.

McLagan, P., and Nel, C. *The Age of Participation.* San Francisco: Berrett-Koehler, 1995.

Mintzberg, H. *The Rise and Fall of Strategic Planning.* New York: The Free Press, 1994.

Norris, D. M., and Morrison, J. L. (eds.). *Mobilizing for Transformation: How Campuses Are Preparing for the Knowledge Age.* New Directions for Institutional Research, no. 4. San Francisco: Jossey-Bass, 1997.

Norris, D. M., and Poulton, N. L. *A Guide for New Planners.* Ann Arbor, Mich.: Society for College and University Planning, 1991.

Schmidtlein, F. A., and Milton, T. H. "College and University Planning Perspectives From a Nation-Wide Study." *Planning for Higher Education,* 1989, 17(3), 1–19.

Schmidtlein, F. A., and Milton, T. H. (eds.). *Adapting Strategic Planning to Campus Realities.* New Directions for Institutional Research, no. 67. San Francisco: Jossey-Bass, 1990.

Sell, K. R., and Moen, D. "Just-In-Time and Strategic Planning: Strategic Budgeting in Public Higher Education at the System and Institution Levels." Paper presented at the Association for Institutional Research Annual Forum, Minneapolis, May 1998.

Vandement, W. E., and Jones, D. P. (eds.). *Financial Management: Progress and Challenges.* New Directions for Higher Education, no. 83. San Francisco: Jossey-Bass, 1993.

Ziegler, S. G. "From Planning to Achieving." *Planning for Higher Education,* 1999, 28(1), 19–28.

PATRICIA N. HAEUSER is director of budget, planning, and analysis at the University of Wisconsin–Stout.

9

Learning is often viewed as that which occurs in the classroom. This chapter examines the profile and profession of a college administrator involved in the other curriculum.

Student Life and Development

Jan Minoru Javinar

One purpose of higher education frequently cited in institutional mission statements and college catalogues is the development of students as well-rounded, whole individuals. The profession of student affairs views this purpose as the reason for its existence in academe. *Student affairs* refers to the administrative unit on a college campus responsible for those out-of-classroom staff members, programs, functions, and services that contribute to the education and development of students.

Overview of Student Affairs

One unique characteristic of U.S. higher education is "its concern for students' personal growth and development in addition to their intellectual advancement" (Rentz and Knock, 1987, p. 1). As a goal or purpose of higher education, the active promotion of the intellectual and *personal* development of students is often referred to as *student development* (Brown, 1986). Another author states that student development as a goal for higher education is the facilitation of the *whole* student's growth (Knock, 1985). The profession of student affairs assumes primary responsibility for the personal and interpersonal development of students.

Until the 1920s, faculty exercised this responsibility until "both the number and the diversity of students increased," at which time specialists who belonged to the emerging field of college student personnel (precursor to the student affairs profession) were assigned (Rentz and Knock, 1987, p. 1). Over time, the practice of student affairs administration has evolved with two approaches: one of service and the other of development. The former approach is concerned with the efficient delivery of programs and services to meet an array of student needs, whereas the latter is concerned with the purposeful design of programs and services to effect desired student outcomes. To be purposeful in their practice, most of the specialty areas within student affairs use both approaches.

Student Life

One specialty area of the student affairs profession is student life or student activities. Student life programs or activities have been part of U.S. higher education throughout history, albeit in different forms (Whipple, 1996). The chronology begins with historical religious activities such as regular prayer, Bible study, and church attendance; continues with literary societies, Greek social organizations, student government associations, student athletics, student union programs, and student organizations with academic, career, cultural, and political interests; and is more recently represented by leadership development programs, peer mentoring, and volunteer service activities. Today, the student life program on a college campus still includes many of the aforementioned types of organizations and activities.

Mission of Student Life. The overall mission of the student life program is to help students become more self-directed in their learning, behavior, and actions to manage their own lives. Because much of what students do in their daily lives involves interactions with others, it is critical that students learn to improve their interpersonal skills and their abilities to work effectively within organizational or group settings.

To fulfill their mission, most student life programs pursue two basic goals: (1) to provide cocurricular programs, activities, and other learning opportunities that contribute to the quality of life for students by meeting their academic, social, recreational, physical, emotional, and moral development needs and (2) to promote self-direction and leadership among those students who become involved in managing student life programs and activities or who assume an active role in campus governance. Inherent in these two goals are both *product* and *process* outcomes of equal importance. Through the delivery of programs, activities, services, and opportunities (the product) that meet the developmental needs of the campus student population, the student life program involves students in organizational governance (the process) that fosters their development of self-direction and leadership.

Functions Performed. Student life professionals perform a triad of functions similar to those of other student affairs professionals: teaching, counseling, and administering. Teaching in student life takes many forms. Among these are credit instruction in leadership and organizational skills open to any and all students; noncredit one-day workshops targeted for student leaders and student organizations; in-service training for student employees or full-time staff; weekend retreats at camps, hotels, and other sites away from the campus; outdoor experiences involving high-risk and low-risk problem-solving tasks known as *group initiatives;* one-on-one training; and research to produce informational materials and handouts on topics related to leadership and organizational development.

Counseling in the student life context is primarily organizational advising rather than counseling in the therapeutic sense. Student life professionals attempt to effect student learning in varied group contexts and settings, including student government, national honor societies, academic or career interest clubs, peer mentoring groups, fraternities and sororities, community service teams, student staff at residence halls, college union work teams, sports clubs, political action groups, and student affairs support groups. Through those activities, student life professionals advise and counsel students in techniques and behaviors that support or promote interpersonal effectiveness including getting along with others, resolving differences, working collaboratively, reaching consensus, visioning common goals, articulating expectations and ideas, and listening for understanding.

The third student affairs function of administering involves the design, delivery, and evaluation of programs and services intended to meet student needs. For student life professionals, the student union facility provides the venue within which such programs and services are offered. The student union serves as the "community center of the college, for all members of the college family—students, faculty, administration, alumni, and guests" (Packwood, 1977, p. 180). Many of the student life services, programs, and amenities are conveniently provided to fulfill the daily needs of campus community members. Among these amenities are "a place to sit between classes, hang one's coat, get a bite to eat, find out what is happening on campus, make a phone call, take a nap, buy a book or supplies, park one's car, or hold a meeting" (p. 181). Other administering functions in student life include student organization registration or recognition, coordination or scheduling of student organization events, supervision of student activity fees, and policy formulation and implementation (McKaig and Policello, 1979).

Organization and Staffing of Student Life. The staffing patterns and service offerings of student life programs are often functions of an institution's size and mission, student enrollment, student demographics, and funding levels, among other variables (Whipple, 1996). Whether a professional coordinates the service offerings on a full-time basis or as a percentage part of her or his job description is affected by the institution's size and type. In larger institutions, several full-time professionals may specialize in one or more service areas, whereas in smaller institutions, a professional may serve as a generalist and perform a little in many service areas.

The chief administrator of student life programs may carry titles such as director of student activities, director of student union, director of student union and student activities, or assistant dean of student life. Depending on institution size and program complexity, the director may report to the senior student affairs officer of the campus, the dean of students, or the director of student union where the student activities program is part of the student union. Directors usually hold a master's degree, and in some cases the director's position may require a doctorate.

Entry-level positions generally hold the titles of program advisors or program coordinators, with either generalist duties at smaller institutions or specialist duties at larger ones. Examples include coordinator of student organization services, leadership development specialist, Greek life advisor, programming board advisor, residential life specialist, student government advisor, student media advisor, student organization business manager, coordinator of multicultural programming, new-student orientation coordinator, leisure recreation program coordinator, and service-learning coordinator. These entry-level positions minimally require a bachelor's degree with designated years of work experience but are increasingly requiring a master's degree. Graduate assistantships in student life areas are generally available as part of a campus's advanced degree program in student affairs administration.

The skills and competencies required of individuals seeking a career in campus activities were identified more than a decade ago by a committee of the National Association for Campus Activities (NACA), one of two major associations of student life professionals working in the field of student activities and student union (Allen, Julian, Stern, and Walborn, 1987). The other major association of student life professionals, the Association of College Unions International (ACUI), is also examining whether core competencies around which preservice and in-service training programs are designed can be identified and agreed to by professionals in the field.

The model posited by NACA consists of a foundation of twenty personal qualities identified as valuable for effective student life professionals. Among these qualities are altruism, cooperativeness, flexibility, sense of hope, sense of humor, sense of professionalism, tolerance, and trustworthiness (Allen, Julian, Stern and Walborn, 1987, pp. 26–29). Building on the foundation of personal qualities is a knowledge base centering around the areas of higher education, college students, social sciences, business administration, leisure studies, and self-understanding (pp. 32–35). The combination of personal qualities and knowledge bases aids student life professionals in acquiring basic and general skills clustered among four areas: task management, process management, resource management, and risk management (pp. 38–44). Research suggests that this model for professional development and job success was useful in identifying factors that influence the professional commitment of student affairs practitioners in the state of Hawai'i to the student development mission of higher education (Javinar, 1997).

Major Challenges and Issues

Student life programs in the twenty-first century remain beset with challenges and issues requiring thoughtful and responsive attention. Internal to the campus community, student life programs must contend with two issues:

their value and worth to the institution and changing student demographics. Externally, major developments in case law may potentially impact the future funding of student life programs as well as the future relationship among students, student organizations, and institutions of higher education.

Value and Worth of Student Life Programs. Despite the programmatic shift toward increased educational services in the form of leadership development and organizational development instruction, the student life program continues to be plagued with campus perceptions that student activities and student union programs are unnecessary frills, ancillary, if not antithetical, to the college mission. Many student life professionals repeatedly hear the surprise in faculty and staff voices that student activities and student union programs are more than landlocked equivalents of cruiseship activities. Challenging the perception that the student life program merely orchestrates a series of discrete and disparate socials, speakers, singers, and frivolous entertainment acts remains critical for practitioners in student life in times of budget shortfalls, retrenchment, and prosperity. To survive and grow, the student life program must demonstrate its contributions to student growth intellectually and interpersonally. Doing so may not only deflect the budget axe but may also increase the willingness of academic departments and other student affairs programs to forge partnerships in creating seamless learning experiences that are educationally and developmentally purposeful. The creation of such partnerships however, remains more easily expressed than enacted.

Changing Student Demographics. Drawing data from the American Council of Education, Stage and Anaya (1996) summarize the changing demographics of U.S. college students. They note a decline in Caucasian students from 90 percent of the college population of first-time, full-time freshmen in 1966 to 81 percent in 1994, while first-time, full-time freshmen who are women increased during the same period from 44 percent to 53 percent. Larger numbers of students of color are entering higher education, with Asian Americans and African Americans showing slow but continuous growth and Native Americans and Hispanics showing steady state enrollments (p. xii). There has also been a decline in traditional-aged, first-time, full-time freshmen (that is, those 18 years of age or younger) from 81 percent in 1966 to 68 percent in 1994. These changing demographics challenge the student life program to reexamine its service and program offerings to ensure responsiveness to needs of students whose culture, ethnicity, gender, and age differ from the college students traditionally and historically served. These demographic changes have been accompanied by other changes. At one university, assessment results using the College Student Experiences Questionnaire (CSEQ) showed that student involvement in campus clubs, organizations, or student government decreased over a nine-year period (Office of Vice President for Student Affairs, 1999, p. 1). Additionally, more students reported working on committees, organizations, or projects off campus than on campus. College matriculation may be more a part-time endeavor than a full-time one, with academics and studying increasingly in competition with off-campus employment, relationships, family, leisure, and other demands. Serving students who have finite time on campus requires creative approaches and may require paradigmatic shifts if student life is to remain viable and relevant. The advent of virtual instruction poses additional challenges to the conventional notions of campus community and community building.

Case Law Developments. Student life programs may be supported by both state and nonstate dollars. *State dollars* are those appropriated through legislative channels including taxpayer support via income and property taxes. *Nonstate dollars* are those fees, commonly referred to as *student activity fees,* that college campuses require students to pay to support such programs as student government, student newspapers, student clubs, student services such as child-care services or health services, and other student organizations. Lawsuits in a number of states are challenging the use of such student activity fees for organizations and groups that espouse views or embrace political actions with which student fee payers disagree. Stipulations by the courts on how student activity fees may be used could curtail the authority of campus student governments and ultimately impair their effectiveness if students can opt to not pay those fees.

Another similar legal trend involves whether campus student publications are covered under constitutional guarantees of free speech. One U.S. Court of Appeals has allowed college administrators in Kentucky to approve or reject the contents of a college yearbook. This trend may potentially allow the content of college newspapers to be subject to prior administrative review, a practice customarily reserved for primary and secondary school administrators, and thus dilute the student newspaper's historical role as a free-speech forum.

Recent alcohol-related deaths among fraternity pledges and members; the murder of an openly gay student in Wyoming; increased political actions taken by racial, ethnic, and cultural minority groups; and overt protests by white supremacist youth organizations present ongoing challenges to the student life profession. Responses included purposefully designed programs, activities, and services to promote student learning about multiculturalism, diversity, tolerance, and appreciation of differences. In short, the student development mission to foster and transform student knowledge, behaviors, feelings, and values through purposeful learning experiences persists as a major challenge.

My Pathway

I was drawn to the field of education early in my life. Little did I know that a profession existed that combined the functions of teaching, counseling, and administering all into one until I learned about student affairs. My passion for student affairs administration in general and for student life administration in particular stems from my sincere conviction in the transformative power of education. I have experienced social mobility because of my journey through academia, earning both master's and doctoral degrees in higher education administration. I am nevertheless more convinced that higher education promotes cognitive upward mobility than it does economic and social upward mobility; this transformative power of higher education is evident when individuals expand their freedom to choose a path, to improve their lot in whatever form desired, and to become increasingly self-directed. This philosophy, coupled with the student development goal of higher education and the variety of tasks required to be performed that inhere in the student affairs triadic functions of teaching, counseling, and administering, continues to reaffirm my career choice in student life and student affairs.

Ever since my freshman year in high school, I knew that I wanted to teach. My inspiration derived from the enthusiasm, passion, and knowledge I saw in my ninth-grade social studies teacher. Her methods of large-group circle discussions, organized debates, current events, simulations, and small-group activities made me keenly aware that one could learn historical facts through methods that engaged and involved students. That spark, coupled with my exposure to student council activities, equipped me with a philosophy of service to others. I continued in class council and student government activities throughout my high school and college years, affirming my belief that service to others gave meaning to my life.

During the summer before my senior year in college, a friend of mine talked about going away for graduate school to study a field I had never heard of, college student services administration (CSSA). So while I prepared myself to join the ranks of unemployed secondary school social studies teachers after college graduation, my friend went off to study CSSA. Because I was willing to teach anywhere in my home state, I was fortunate to secure public school teaching jobs in social studies immediately after graduating with my bachelor's degree in secondary education teaching. But positions were scarce, so for each of the three years that I taught social studies, I was at a different school. This tested my commitment to teach and taught me to become flexible, versatile, and adaptive to change.

All the time I worked as a public school teacher, I enrolled in one graduate course each semester, desiring to be and do the best that I could. Even after I left public school teaching to pursue management training in a savings and loan institution, I continued enrolling in graduate courses in curriculum development. I eventually switched to educational administration courses as a way to psychologically justify my time away from the savings and loan office while attending graduate school.

After two years in private industry, I accepted my first full-time position in higher education, working with educationally and economically disadvantaged high school juniors and seniors to prepare them for acceptance into a four-year college or university. By the time I graduated with my master's degree, I had worked in two federally funded projects in higher education, one with the high school juniors and seniors and the other with ethnically diverse, language-minority students interested in teaching in the public schools. Both of these jobs honed my advising skills as well as my administrative abilities to manage an office, design systems of delivery, execute and monitor a budget, and maintain student records. Additionally, I was able to refine my teaching through noncredit workshops in learning skills, career explorations, and college financial aid and admissions processes. In short, I was called upon and learned to perform the student affairs triad of functions early on in my career.

I spent the next three years as a community college student affairs professional working first as a financial aid administrator and a student employment coordinator, and later in student activities administration, which included supervising a health nurse. It was at the community college that I was introduced to the potential of student activities to reduce the attrition rate of college students. Through a major student affairs divisional reorganization that I helped to effect, student activities made an intentional philosophical shift with a name change to *student life and development* and with programmatic changes to include added service offerings in health and wellness education, new student orientation, leadership development, and campus center services. During these years at the community college, I developed my supervisory skills and approach, working initially with clerical staff then progressing to a nonfaculty professional.

In 1988, I transferred from my community college position as director of student life and development to assume a position as the associate director of student activities at the flagship campus of the University of Hawai'i system. Over the last five years, I have served as the director of the department, first on an interim basis for two years and since then as permanent director. I find that being the director not only affords me opportunities to promote and foster the development of students as well-rounded, whole individuals but also presents me with daily moments to do the same with the individual staff members with whom I work. It is through these opportunities that I employed the transformative power of higher education.

References

Allen, K. E., Julian, F. H., Stern, C. M., and Walborn, N.C. *Future Perfect: A Guide for Professional Development and Competence.* Columbia, S.C.: National Association for Campus Activities Educational Foundation, 1987.

Brown, R. D. "Editorial." *Journal of College Student Personnel,* 1986, 27(1), 3.

Javinar, J. M. "Towards Purposeful Practices in Student Affairs: An Exploratory Study of the Profession in the State of Hawai'i." Unpublished doctoral dissertation, University of Hawai'i at Mānoa, 1997.

Knock, G. H. "Development of Student Services in Higher Education." In M. J. Barr, L. A. Keating, and Associates (eds.), *Developing Effective Student Services Programs: Systematic Approaches for Practitioners.* San Francisco: Jossey-Bass, 1985.

McKaig, R. N., and Policello, S. M. "Student Activities." In G. D. Kuh (ed.), *Evaluation in Student Affairs.* Cincinnati, Ohio: American College Personnnel Association (ACPA), 1979.

Office for the Vice President for Student Affairs. *College Student Experiences at the University of Hawai'i at Mānoa in 1990, 1993, 1996, and 1999.* University of Hawai'i at Mānoa, Aug. 1999.

Packwood, W. T. "Union." In W. T. Packwood (ed.), *College Student Personnel Services.* Springfield, Ill.: Charles C. Thomas, 1977.

Rentz, A. L., and Knock, G. H. *Careers in the College Student Personnel Profession.* Alexandria, Va.: American College Personnel Association (ACPA) Media, 1987.

Stage, F. K., and Anaya, G. L. "A Transformational View of College Student Research." In F. K. Stage and others (eds.), *College Students: The Evolving Nature of Research.* Needham Heights, Mass.: Simon & Schuster, 1996.

Whipple, E. G. "Student Activities." In A. L. Rentz and Associates (eds.), *Student Affairs Practice in Higher Education.* (2nd ed.) Springfield, Ill.: Charles C. Thomas, 1996.

JAN MINORU JAVINAR is director of cocurricular activities, programs and services at University of Hawai'i at Mānoa and serves as an adjunct instructor in student affairs administration for the department of educational administration.

10

The author provides one model for structuring business affairs within academic administration.

Academic Business Affairs

Larry M. Dooley

U.S. colleges and universities are most paradoxical in that it is said that they constitute one of the largest industries in the nation but are among the least business-like and most poorly managed of all organizations (Keller, 1983). The differences between academic institutions and business firms are significant enough that systems of coordination and control effective in one of these types of organizations might not be expected to have the same effect in the other. Leading a group of individuals who are all well educated and, for the most part, intellectually equal is very different from managing a group of individuals in an organization with stratified staffing (Dooley, 1989).

The days of amateur administration, when faculty temporarily assumed administrative positions and then returned to the classroom, are long since over at most institutions. Department heads and deans continue to come from the faculty ranks, and they are given the responsibility for the administration of units that include student affairs, faculty concerns, and financial affairs operations. As institutions become larger and more complex, knowledge of legal precedents, federal regulations, management information systems, student financial aid procedures, grant and contract administration, and many other areas of specialized expertise is needed to accomplish these administrative tasks.

The importance of academic business administration within the colleges and departments of a university cannot be taken lightly. Effective business operations in a university provide the means of ensuring order and

The author would like to acknowledge the assistance of Deborah Buckley, assistant dean for finance and administration for the College of Education, and Barry Nelson, vice president for finance and business services, Texas A & M University System Health Science Center.

economy in educational activities. Business administrators are colleagues of the faculty, and they should share the same larger aims (Dooley, 1991). Thus, the role of the academic business administrator is to place administrative work in an educational context: to relate decisions and procedures to the colleges and department within the academic community, to note points where adherence or subservience to general rules may help or hinder the institution's academic progress, and especially to emphasize those regions where administrative decisions are useful and indeed indispensable. It is critical that these administrative decision makers understand the colleges and departments where most academic decisions are made.

The Problem

In the 1970s, universities experienced rapid transformation. Some moved from delegating business and finance duties to academic administrators such as deans and department heads to realizing the necessity to assign these duties to business-trained professionals. Other universities, however, remain committed to leaving this responsibility to faculty in administrative roles.

Academic executives and faculty form separate and isolated conclaves in which they are likely to communicate only with people similar to themselves (Rourke and Brooks, 1964). In an attempt to bridge this gap in 1979, Texas A & M University, following a model initiated by Purdue, established the position of senior academic business administrator (SABA) to reduce or alleviate widespread inconsistency and inefficiency in the administration of academic business operations. All ten academic colleges and the university library hired individuals for these newly formed positions. For adoption of the program to be complete, the decision to create these positions in each college was not optional. Moreover, the funding for these positions came from central administration. The academic colleges included Architecture, Business, Education, Geosciences, Liberal Arts, Science, Veterinary Medicine, Agriculture, and Engineering. Over time, the decision was made to place these positions only in the academic colleges; positions were not created in the division of Rural Public Health, the Health Science Center, or the George Bush School of Public Affairs.

Description of the Position

SABA is a midlevel position, reporting to the dean of each academic college and with direct communications to the office of the executive vice president and provost. The position is intended to relieve the deans of business management duties and to reduce inconsistency and inefficiency in academic business operations. There are two levels of the position (SABA I or SABA II) depending on several factors such as size of the college budget, number of faculty, enrollment, number of student credit hours typically generated, and the amount of contract and grant funding.

The tasks and responsibilities of a SABA include working closely with department heads and the dean in the coordinating and monitoring of the budget process; monitoring and signing all payroll documents for the college; evaluating financial reports for each of the departments and reporting to the dean; monitoring books on all general revenue accounts, discretionary accounts, and research accounts; conducting monthly training and informational meetings for all departmental academic business administrators and departmental bookkeepers; interpreting and advising the college concerning university policies and procedures; reviewing and approving all nonacademic positions—hiring, terminations, salary adjustments, and promotions; coordinating college and university reports (for example, affirmative action, teaching load, and space allocation); and serving as a member of the college's executive team.

In the beginning, subsequent to the hiring decisions at Texas A & M, each SABA completed an intensive eighteen-hour training program that carried him or her through each division of university operations from the business office to the motor pool and the university-owned airport. Not only did the training cover all relevant policies and procedures, but it also introduced the SABA to the decision makers in each of these areas within the university community. Such contacts within the university network are invaluable.

Although no formal training currently exists for the SABA position, a great deal of networking has taken place at monthly meetings. The SABAs have been instrumental in spearheading human resource and budget-related policy changes. The SABAs also provide training workshops for departmental academic business administrators.

Path to the Position

The path taken to the SABA position in the beginning was very different from the current trend. In the beginning, the only requirement was a bachelor of business administration (BBA) or related degree and five to six years of supervisory experience. In the twenty years since the inception of the position, there have been several SABAs with Ph.D. degrees; one has a law degree, and the balance have had master's degrees.

The SABA position is a solid and prestigious midlevel position on campus—one that is highly sought when vacancies occur. In academic colleges, the position is the most senior staff position; there is no upward mobility, however, within the academic colleges. As is typical in the academic culture, the positions of assistant and associate dean are reserved for faculty.

Staffing

Within the overall structure of college-level business administration, there may also be an academic business administrator (ABA) who reports directly to the department head. The structure at Texas A & M allows for ABAs in each department; however, funding must come from the department (unlike the funding for SABAs, which comes from the central administration). As daily business operations are becoming more sophisticated, the need for departments to create these positions is outweighing the financial burden; more and more ABA positions are being created in addition to the clerical and secretarial support already there. In fact, more and more departments are opting for ABAs, as rules, regulations, and the complexity of the job must be dealt with daily.

As noted, no upward mobility exists for the SABA unless one would be interested in moving to the central business office, and often this is not considered an upward move. SABAs generally do not want to move to the university business office because either they do not want to leave the academic side of the house or they appreciate the fact that in the college they are considered to be the senior staff members. Moving from an environment where one is the senior staff member to one where you are one of many is considered a lateral move, at best. To attain a senior staff position in the business office would also require a certified public accountant credential, which is not required, and few in the colleges possess one.

Although mobility is somewhat limited, individuals have moved to such positions as assistant dean, assistant provost, and director of research since the creation of these positions. As a solution to the mobility issue, the current SABA group has proposed a career ladder for this position that has four levels beginning with a position at the departmental level and ascending to the dean level (business assistant, business associate, business specialist, and business administrator). It is believed that if universities were to adopt these titles, a true career ladder would exist and provide opportunities for advancement and upward mobility.

For the ABA positions, a bachelor degree is required, and no equivalent experience is accepted for the degree. Upward mobility for the ABAs means moving into the SABA position. This frequently occurs when vacancies open across campus. Individuals in the ABA positions produce a rich talent pool when SABA positions become vacant.

There is virtually no movement by senior academic administrators from college to college. It takes time to develop trust with the dean and the faculty of the college, and if SABAs were to leave for another college position, they would have to rebuild their credibility and trust with the dean.

Major Functional Challenges

The SABA group has emerged over time to be considered by the university community as the movers and shakers within a college unit. They originate most of the policy changes and other streamlining efforts relating to academic colleges. An example of such issues include development of on-line budgeting for the university, position and job title problems with accompanying low pay scale, a financial aid process information packet, automated payroll processing, faculty and staff salary increase forms, and training needs for business personnel (training workshops with concurrent sessions for all business personnel on campus are sponsored quarterly by this group). Many of these examples may appear elementary and simple; however, the fact is that these tasks have now been accomplished, and there was no champion for these efforts until the SABA group was established. Many of these efforts to increase efficiency resulted in substantial savings to the departments and the university.

Professional Challenges

The challenges for these positions in the middle role are conveyed in this scenario: "The plight of many middle managers in higher education is not unlike that of Snoopy in a 'Peanuts' cartoon. Snoopy lies on the ground saying, 'Yesterday I was a dog, today I am a dog.' Then, walking along, he thinks, 'Tomorrow morning I will still be a dog.' Sighing, he stops and ponders, 'So little hope for progress'" (Kraus, 1983, p. 29).

Recognition and appreciation for the position have made much progress. These positions are viewed as having considerable power and influence on campus. Because they are housed in the academic unit or college, they have the full support and influence of the deans, which allows them considerable respect within the business community on campus. When vacancies occur in these positions, the number of applicants is usually quite high, both from internal campus positions as well as from external sources. It is not unusual to recruit nationally. There is no question that the SABA positions have been highly successful in providing administrative support to the deans. This is a successful model that may be adopted by other universities of similar size and structure.

Professional Development

Much of the opportunity for career and professional development is created by these administrators themselves. The one organization that serves business administrators is the National Association of College and University Business Officers. Even this organization is not a perfect fit because issues discussed include areas outside the purview of college-based administrators such as physical plant operations, institutional planning, and internal audits. It is, however, the closest organization. The other possibility is the human resources organization—College and University Personnel Association. Because SABAs in some ways are eclectic in the areas they cover, most attend both of these organizations and select the topics they need because no one association is devoted entirely to academic business administration.

The one best way for development in this group of employees is informal networking. Prior to the advent of e-mail, informal networking was not as simple. Major obstacles encountered by an individual SABA are now communicated easily, and intervention strategies are created to inform others of the situation. No formal ongoing training exists for this group with the exception of information sharing from the different vice president's offices at monthly meetings.

Trends in the Field

For an institution of higher education to function in a manner consistent with the expectations of stakeholders, there must be perceived integrity and fidelity to the institution's mission and processes. Given the complexity of higher education cultures, the ability to manage the academic institution and adapt or change in light of the information age—and at the same time retain systemic integrity—is a critical challenge facing academic administration (Nelson, 1999). It would be very difficult to attend to this task without the support and the expertise of positions similar to that of the SABA.

Purdue University, Florida State University, and the University of Texas all have models similar to that described here; however, in two of these cases, the SABA reports to the vice president for finance and not to the deans, and the program is not required to be in each college. To the knowledge of this researcher, no other models exist nationally similar to these. With business operations becoming more complex and diverse and college units increasingly required to generate their own resource base, models such as these should be considered. There have been two research studies to date examining the effectiveness of the senior academic business administrator model: one by Dooley (1991) and another by Nelson (1999). Further research should be conducted to examine the effectiveness of generalizing this model to other institutional types and sizes. Why has this model not been adopted by other universities? One can speculate. Faculty have always managed these tasks; why change? It is often assumed that staff cannot understand the needs and desires of faculty or that they will never gain the confidence of the faculty. It is true that the SABA must be able to straddle two cultures: the academic and the nonacademic. The example provided here demonstrates that such a position can be managed with considerable benefit to the institution.

My Career Path

I began my career as the first person to hold the SABA position within the college of education, and I held it for sixteen years. I began my career in this position with a bachelor of science degree and four years' experience after college. I began working on a master's degree part time and completed it in three years; my doctorate was completed, also while working full time, in four and one half years. Subsequent to receiving my doctoral degree, one of the departments in the college hired me to teach a course in procurement and management of contracts and grants because of my experience in assisting faculty in procurement and my leadership in the post-award process. During this time, the department conducted a national search for a new faculty, and I was fortunate enough to be the unanimous choice of the search committee. I began my tenure-track position, again while working full time as the SABA for the college of education. After my three-year evaluation it became very clear that I could no longer handle both positions and have any real expectation of being awarded tenure, so I resigned my position and became a full-time faculty member.

Due to my administrative experience within academic business administration, I have held the positions of interim director of the Center for Distance Learning Research and assistant department head. I currently hold the position of associate professor and interim department head. It is highly unusual at most universities for an individual to hold the position of department head without the rank of professor. There is no question in my mind that I would not have been considered for the department head position were it not for the experience I gained as the SABA.

References

Dooley, L. M. "The Senior Academic Business Administrator at Texas A & M University: A Comparative Study of a Single Personnel Intervention." Journal for Higher Education Management, 1991, 7(1), 3–10.

Keller, G. American Strategy: The Management Revolution in Higher Education. Baltimore: Johns Hopkins University Press, 1983.

Kraus, J. D., Jr. "Middle Management in Higher Education: A Dog's Life?" Journal of the College and University Personnel Association, 1983, 34(4), 29–34.

Nelson, B. C. "The Senior Academic Business Administrator at Texas A & M University: A Study of a Single Personnel Intervention." Unpublished doctoral dissertation, Department of Educational Administration, Texas A & M University, 1999.

Rourke, F. E., and Brooks, G. E. "The Managerial Revolution in Higher Education." Administrative Science Quarterly, 1964, 9(2), 154–181.

LARRY M. DOOLEY is associate professor and interim department head of educational human resource development, College of Education, Texas A & M University, College Station, Texas.

11

Although the practice of Institutional Research may have much to do with the production of data, the art is contextualizing that data, converting it to information, and making it meaningful.

Institutional Research

Deborah Olsen

There has never been a better time to consider institutional research (IR) as a field. Over the past thirty years, IR has solidified and enhanced its role within institutions of higher education and better articulated itself as a professional community nationally. As Peterson (1985) predicted, IR has evolved with the changing needs of higher education and has become associated with the advanced technical and statistical competencies that are the cornerstone of our burgeoning information culture. As colleges and universities struggle to meet increasingly complex and intrusive reporting requirements, to plan more effectively in a highly competitive educational market, and to make the best use of new multimillion-dollar computer systems, they are expanding existing IR offices or creating new ones. By discussing IR as it was and is, I hope to also shed some light on what it will become as the new century unfolds as well as the rich potential that IR holds for individual careers and for higher education as a whole.

Some History

IR offices began to emerge in the early 1960s, largely as a means of complying with state and federal reporting requirements. In addition to mandated reports, data requests from nongovernmental sources (such as accreditation associations and higher education organizations) were growing as well, both in number and complexity. From these humble beginnings, IR offices began to grow and diversify, shaped largely by institutional characteristics such as size and type of institutional control, public or private—factors still very much in evidence today (Delaney, 1997). Perhaps as important as these more tangible factors, however, was the decision-making style of the president and upper-level administrators, that is, whether they

NEW DIRECTIONS FOR HIGHER EDUCATION, no. 111, Fall 2000 © Jossey-Bass, a Wiley company

were data driven in their approach to issues and planning. Although external requirements were sufficient to encourage many institutions to dedicate some resources to ensure compliance with basic reporting needs, it was the internal institutional value placed on information and data that often determined the scope and nature of IR's responsibilities. At the risk of sounding like an economic determinist, it is worth noting that fiscally, the 1970s and early to mid-1980s were a period of significant and sustained growth in higher education. In a more forgiving fiscal environment, there was not the same premium on information as in a highly constrained environment where even relatively minor errors in planning and decision making can have a substantial impact on institutional well-being.

Through the 1980s and 1990s shock waves of change ran through the higher education community. Major changes in state and federal policy ranged from increased oversight of campus financial aid dollars to reductions in state funding for public higher education to greater accountability for such diverse issues as graduation rates and campus safety. The market of eighteen-year-old applicants shrunk over part of this period as tuition costs continued to soar well above national cost-of-living increases. High schools produced record numbers of graduates with A and B grade point averages, while colleges and universities reported a significant and costly growth in remedial courses. Greater numbers of professional support staff, higher faculty salaries, and enormous new technology costs (largely unbudgeted) strained institutional budgets. In response, colleges and universities reallocated funds and even began to downsize faculty, staff, and programs. Whether the long-term consequences of such significant change will be to revitalize or hamper higher education is not yet clear. Much will depend on postsecondary education's response. What is clear, however, is that virtually every one of the events cited here has increased the value of information to institutions of higher education. Moreover, it is no longer sufficient for institutions to know only their own inner processes, resources, and goals; they must understand the social, political, and economic currents shaping the society at large and the external constituencies they serve in particular to be successful.

What Is IR?

Although there is no commonly agreed-upon definition of IR, Peterson and Corcoran (1985) conceive of IR as research designed to generate information that serves planning, policy development, resource allocation, and management or evaluation decisions in all functional areas). In a similar vein, Fincher could confidently refer to IR as "organizational intelligence" or "a professional technical specialty with strong resources and capabilities for policy related research in institutions of higher education" (cited in Terenzini, 1993, p. 3). A far cry from simple reporting responsibilities, this definition argues for IR as a profession with a coherent and identifiable set of professional competencies. Moreover, Fincher and others assert that despite its technical core, the professional practice of IR is as much art as science. In a more recent article, Terenzini (1993) describes IR as based on three interdependent kinds of organizational intelligence: (1) *technical and analytical intelligence,* which includes factual information as well as analytical and methodological skills; (2) *issues intelligence,* which ensures an understanding of the substantive problems to be addressed and the politics and procedures associated with institutional processes and decision making; and (3) *contextual intelligence,* which involves understanding the culture of higher education locally and nationally. As Terenzini puts it, contextual intelligence "is the crowning form of organizational intelligence, dependent upon the other two tiers but lifting them out of a preoccupation with topically relevant data and specific analytical tools. It makes possible the prudent, intelligent, and illuminating application of technical and methodological intelligence to locally meaningful versions of general issues. . . . It is the form of intelligence that earns institutional researchers legitimacy, trust and respect" (p. 6). Thus, although the *practice* of IR may have much to do with the production of data, the *art* is contextualizing that data, converting it to information, and making it meaningful.

Chan (1993) makes the argument that IR coevolves with the planning processes of colleges and universities. According to Chan, as planning processes mature and become more strategic, the institutional reference point shifts from "internal contexts (e.g., faculty, program, students, facilities) to its external contexts (e.g., changes in demographic trends, market competition, regional and local economy, technological advancement, student aid policies)" (p. 534). Further development occurs when the institution moves from strategic planning to strategic management, which integrates the focus on the internal and the external in a single planning framework created by the institution. The framework reaffirms institutional culture and values while recognizing that the institution may need to reposition itself to accomplish its goals in a changing environment. This final planning phase is more proactive than prior phases and channels institutional energies into shaping the future as well as predicting it. Although the radical changes of recent years have encouraged many schools to move to more strategic planning processes, few, if any, employ strategic management according to Chan.

The corollaries for IR are fairly direct. Pre-strategic planning focuses on "descriptive analysis of institutional components" (Chan, 1993, p. 537). Thus, institutions count students for federal reports or conduct alumni surveys for assessment and accreditation. Little attempt is made to apply data to institutional issues or even to integrate the different pieces of data collected. Historical trends are of interest because we assume the future will be like the past. As external forces impinge more forcefully on institutional function, however, our ability to understand the effects of these forces on our institutions becomes critical. Analysis becomes more complex and predictive, attempting to assess the risks and opportunities inherent in different situations; the focus is on issues now rather than the data per se. And finally, as institutions begin to move into strategic management, IR begins to relate external variables to the institution's culture and values. A more holistic approach to the data is taken, and researchers work to synthesize a wide array of data into a planning framework that represents both "intuition and rigorous analysis" (Chan, 1993, p. 538).

In this vein, it is worth noting that there are some very important differences between applied and basic academic research and that these prove to be either a positive or a negative depending on the individual's temperament and goals. Applied research, such as IR, has immediate implications for organizations, for the people who work for them, and for how they utilize money and resources. Mistakes matter, and they often matter right away. This is not a field for the risk averse. Applied research is often done under fairly tight time constraints. Decisions will be made with or without information. It is better to have the best information available than no information at all. This is not a field for those who have difficulty prioritizing tasks and who cannot work within limits that others set. And last, the primary consumer of the information generated (in other words, the people who pay you to produce it) are not your academic peers but administrators, trustees, and even legislators. The audience is intelligent, but they are not necessarily fellow social scientist and statisticians. The research carried out should meet the methodological and technical standards of the academic discipline, but the presentation should make these standards transparent to the decision makers who are the target audience—often a difficult balancing act.

Institutional Researchers of Tomorrow: Skills and Training Needed

I believe that the enhanced stature of the profession and the greater rewards it offers will encourage new recruits to choose IR as a career far more deliberately and self-consciously. In turn, far more will be expected of these recruits in terms of training and expertise. As the Terenzini model (1993) indicates, institutional researchers will continue to need a solid corpus of technical and methodological skills. New technologies place more demands on this basic skill set, not less. In addition to basic programming languages or statistical software such as SPSS and SAS, institutional researchers must be familiar with a variety of other software products and computing tools, for example, spreadsheets, graphics packages, database conversion and transmittal software, hypertext markup language, and Java. In addition, institutional researchers must understand older mainframe environments as well as newer relational databases and distributed computing environments, which are the backbone of the new multimillion-dollar computer systems such as PeopleSoft and Banner. The factual content that Terenzini (1993,

p. 3) describes as part of the first tier of "organizational intelligence" has become more complex as well. Federal and state reporting categories have undergone and continue to undergo considerable change as the government attempts to capture more accurately the heterogeneity of U.S. higher education. New reporting requirements (for example, the requirement that we now track students who should have their financial aid withdrawn mid-semester for nonattendance or the requirement that we track and report incidents of campus violence) challenge institutional researchers to tap previously unused data sources, to reconceptualize old data sources in new ways, or to create data collection mechanisms where none were before. The on-the-job training that many current researchers received will no longer be adequate, given the relative sophistication of even the most basic reporting tasks. As Terenzini suggests, the best way to acquire the technical and substantive knowledge essential to IR is through formal coursework. Courses in statistics, research methods, and the use of different software packages will help novice researchers develop a basic skill set. Graduate-level courses in IR and planning offered by many graduate programs of higher education can be instrumental in linking together the various facets of IR and demonstrating how they are employed in the typical work of such offices—enrollment projections, workload analysis, salary studies, assessment, strategic planning, and so on. Thus, although there is no formal program of study for IR, the academic areas that need to be mastered can be articulated with some specificity.

Terenzini goes on to say that the next level of organizational intelligence, which he calls issues intelligence, can be gained through a combination of coursework and experience, with somewhat more emphasis on formal courses. The coursework cited here includes such topics as the history and philosophy of higher education, curriculum design, organizational analysis, higher education finance, and the impact of college on students. Many of my cohort had not taken these courses when embarking upon their career; some may never had even heard of them. Beginning with little more than research and statistical skills gained through training in some other discipline, such as a social science, many of us pieced together the larger picture of higher education and our institution's place in it through our own reading and study. As the external pressures on higher education have mounted, however, the issues facing it have escalated in scope, complexity, and weight. Today even the greenest of new recruits to IR will need to understand a good deal about higher education, its finances, its students, its governance, and its organization to conduct the kind of research and analysis the institution needs.

Chan (1993) argues that as institutions become more attuned to the external environment, they begin to plan more strategically for the future. IR, in turn, uses modeling and other sophisticated analytical tools to better understand and predict the interaction of internal and external forces. As helpful as the statistical tools are, though, they will have little utility unless institutional researchers know enough about the general issues in higher education to construct models responsive to and to communicate results in terms of these issues. Both Volkwein (1990) and Delaney (1997) have found that the nature of the work performed by the IR office is highly correlated with the educational degrees attained by the staff. These findings not only underscore the importance of formal educational preparation for work in IR but also suggest that more specialized degrees may be required in the future as the field evolves from a technical expertise to a true decision-support function.

Structure and Staffing

In contrast to campus offices with substantial operational responsibility such as the registrar, admissions, and payroll, the IR office tends to be smaller and flatter. IR staff are likely to have masters or doctoral degrees and to hold high-level professional, administrative, or faculty positions. Although larger units may have three or four tiers within the organization, with a director at the head, often there is often not much of career ladder within the immediate IR group. This may change with time and development, but the current organizational structure does have some distinct advantages as well as liabilities. On the positive side, IR offices tend to be small and smart. This enables the unit to work with a minimum of administrative overhead and to be flexible in its response to institutional requests. On the downside, talented staff who work their way up the ranks often find no real upward mobility past a certain point and that they will need to relocate to another college or to another unit within the same college to advance their career. Impressionistically, IR offices appear to be among the first to welcome women and people of color. Speaking from my own experience, I have been able to hire from a talented pool that includes a substantial number of women and people of color. An important question on the horizon is whether women and minorities, once hired, will have access to leadership positions. Recognition in IR, as in many of the midlevel offices, can be difficult to secure. A key challenge for any IR director is obtaining tangible and intangible rewards for staff and doing so in an equitable and meaningful way.

IR offices report to a wide variety of offices: the president, provost, vice provost, dean, and associate or assistant deans. IR may report through academic affairs, but affiliations with student affairs are also common. Although the information needs of higher education have generally had a salutary effect on the standing of IR within institutions, the administrative affiliation of the office is still an important determinant of its role in local decision making; life in an IR office can be frustrating when information generated at considerable expense and effort goes unused and unheeded. However, it is extremely important to use such occasions to assess how responsive an IR office is to the needs, priorities, and politics of the larger institutional context. Individuals interested in IR can formally prepare for its practice, but much of the art will still be acquired through actual experience. IR staff must learn to be not only good stewards of the data they possess but also good brokers of the information they produce.

Professional Organizations

Perhaps because it has been a fledgling field and perhaps because IR offices tend to be small and colleagues far apart, the Association of Institutional Research (AIR) has been a particularly strong and supportive organization. AIR sponsors conferences at both the national and regional level, in addition to various workshops and institutes. AIR has a wide spectrum of publications: newsletters on topical issues; updates on changes in reporting requirements; a primer on IR; the Jossey-Bass series, *New Directions in Institutional Research;* and the journal, *Research in Higher Education.* The association is an invaluable aid for anyone in the field, providing a wealth of information and a network of knowledgeable and helpful colleagues. For anyone interested in IR, participation in AIR is a must. Other professional organizations concerned with higher education can also contribute to the professional development of institutional researchers. The Association for the Study of Higher Education (ASHE) showcases some of the best research on higher education at its annual conference each year. Although ASHE is not as applied as AIR in its research focus, much of the important theoretical and empirical work undergirding higher education scholarship has come from its membership. Many of the same benefits can be derived from Division J of the American Educational Research Association, which represents the higher education track within the larger study of education. The Society for College and University Planners (SCUP) offers another venue for institutional researchers, especially those with an interest in facilities, budgeting, and planning processes. Finally, an increasing number of institutional researchers have been enlisted into the ranks of EDUCAUSE, a rapidly growing association that is at the crossroads of education and technology, highlighting the role that technology plays in all aspects of the educational endeavor.

My Experience in IR

I have discussed the trends in IR and in higher education more generally at some length because they have an enormous impact on the mission of IR offices and the kinds of skills institutional researchers need, today and as the field develops in the near future. I do believe that the field is at a watershed and that individuals who wish to pursue a career in IR will have to prepare more carefully and formally than did many of my cohort. I first worked in an IR office at Ithaca College while still a doctoral student in developmental psychology at Cornell University. My graduate program had provided me with a solid background in quantitative methods and social science research techniques. Moreover, my area of specialization was cognitive development in later adolescence and early adulthood, and although there was little direct application of my academic work to my work in IR, it was useful in establishing context and meaning for some of the findings I generated. In my work as a research analyst, I experienced what was in many ways the best of all situations: the office worked closely with the president of a midsized, highly enterprising school. The office worked intimately and amicably with other key offices, namely, the registrar, financial aid, admissions, and provost, often meeting daily over issues of concern. The campus was extremely sensitive to the external environment, especially as it impacted enrollments, and the office was asked to take on a wider and more sophisticated range of tasks than was typical in many similar offices. And finally, the director was highly supportive of the staff's professional development.

Despite the fact that my experience in IR was quite positive, I still did not identify it as my long-term career objective. I found I enjoyed many things, and it took me some time to identify a career path or skill set I wished to pursue. Over the next several years I worked for a marketing research firm, completed a postdoctoral fellowship in social policy and a child development, served as a graduate practicum director in sociology, and worked as director of faculty development. I finally became director of institutional research at Indiana University after my experiences there and elsewhere helped me articulate what it was about this seemingly disparate set of experiences I valued, enjoyed, and found consistently rewarding. First, research—the collection, analysis, and presentation of data—was the central and guiding activity in all these enterprises. Second, I found myself challenged and engaged when I had to convert data into a meaningful story. I liked presenting research to a variety of audiences with different backgrounds and expertise. In particular, I found the immediate translation of my findings into recommendations for policy or other action quite motivating. But perhaps most of all I liked the continual barrage of new problems and the constant problem solving that came my way as I was given more and more responsibility for different real-world research endeavors. I found I was learning all the time, gathering material, synthesizing, and using it. I was working simultaneously at multiple levels from the detailed and the technical to the global and conceptual. Had I been introduced to IR primarily as a reporting function, it would have generated little enthusiasm. It was finally the opportunities for mastery of new topics and new methods, the need to solve new problems every day, and the feeling that the problems and their solutions mattered that drew me to IR as a field.

References

Chan, S. S. "Changing Roles of Institutional Research in Strategic Management." *Research in Higher Education,* 1993, *34*(5), 533–549.

Delaney, A. M. "The Role of Institutional Research in Higher Education: Enabling Researchers to Meet New Challenges." *Research in Higher Education,* 1997, *38*(1), 1–16.

Peterson, M. W. " Institutional Research: An Evolutionary Perspective." In M.W. Peterson and M. Corcoran (eds.), *Institutional Research in Transition.* New Directions for Institutional Research, no. 46. San Francisco: Jossey-Bass, 1985.

Peterson, M. W., and Corcoran, M. (ed.). *Institutional Research in Transition.* New Directions for Institutional Research, no. 46. San Francisco: Jossey-Bass, 1985.

Terenzini, P. T. "On the Nature of Institutional Research and the Knowledge and Skills It Requires." *Research in Higher Education,* 1993, *34*(1), 117–124.

Volkwein, J. F. "The Diversity of Institutional Research Structures and Tasks." In J. B. Presley (ed.), *Organizing Effective Institutional Research Offices.* New Directions for Institutional Research, no. 66. San Francisco: Jossey-Bass, 1990.

DEBORAH OLSEN *is director of the Office of Institutional Research and Planning Analysis at Virginia Tech University.*

12

Midlevel administrators are critical to the quality and vitality of the academic enterprise.

Commentary

Linda K. Johnsrud

The midlevel administrators who authored the preceding ten chapters well represent the talent, integrity, and insight characteristic of midlevel administrators in colleges and universities. Their pride in their professionalism and their contributions to their institutions are evident. It is important to note that these are not the only midlevel administrative units in higher education. We could have profiled many more; for example, as Huddleston points out in his chapter on enrollment management, there are seven typical units within this function, and each could be headed by a midlevel administrator (for example, directors of admissions, financial aid, registrar, marketing, orientation, and so on). Similarly, within student life and development, as described by Javinar, we could have included housing or career planning and placement. Nonetheless, the ten units described here convey the breadth and richness of the career possibilities in higher education administration.

Despite the significant differences in the substance of their professional roles and responsibilities, the profiles offered by these eleven authors present commonalties that deserve comment. In Rosser's review of the literature, she notes three sources of frustration typical to midlevel administrators as a group: the midlevel nature of their roles, the lack of recognition they receive for their contributions, and the lack of opportunity for career development and advancement. Although there are echoes of these frustrations in the chapters, what is most clear are the positive and proactive responses these administrators take to address these frustrations.

For example, several authors speak to the need for legitimacy of their function within the academic community. Each of the functions described in these chapters is a support function; that is, these administrators provide support to the primary functions of higher education: teaching, research, and service. Dooley, in the chapter on business and finance, and Julius, in the chapter on human resources, both explicitly speak to the gap between the academic and nonacademic sides of the house. Both authors describe the need to work effectively with faculty and the difficulty of doing so, but they also provide effective solutions. In the case of the academic business administrator, the solution offered is structural; Dooley advocates the positioning of the business administrator in the academic college to ensure that the business functions are carried out with close knowledge of academic needs and priorities. Julius advocates that those interested in human resources get the credentials that are valued in higher education and, when in the position, that they attend to both academic and nonacademic human resource issues. Similarly, Tuttle recommends that those who aspire to directorships in academic advising get a doctorate to enhance their credibility with the faculty. Kozobarich, in her chapter on institutional advancement, suggests that fundraisers may have the toughest job in establishing their legitimacy in the academic culture. She characterizes the perceptions of some faculty as suspicious and dismissive and then counters with the need to convey that raising money requires teamwork between the professionals and the faculty and the need for the professionals to work as hard at relations internal to the institution as they do to those external to the institution. In a similar vein, Javinar, in his description of student life and development, speaks to the need for building partnerships with the faculty to demonstrate that the role played by those in student life is supportive of, and not antithetical to, the primary mission of higher education.

The quest for legitimacy pervades these chapters, but those sentiments are accompanied by equally strong statements about the importance of professional development and growth for administrators. It is clear that the professional associations cited in these pages play vital roles in these midlevel administrators' excellence and commitment to their careers. The institutions in which these midlevel administrators work undoubtedly value their contributions, but that fact is not made evident as often as it should be. Thus, it is outside of the institution, among their professional colleagues, that these administrators find opportunities for professional recognition, training and skill development, and networking. Several authors mention the role that professional associations play in preparing entry-level practitioners for advancement. Lassner, in his chapter on information technology (IT), describes the particular difficulty of moving from technical positions to managerial positions in IT. Haeuser describes the same difficulty of combining content or technique with people and political skill when moving up in the planning and budget arena. This difficulty is, in fact, legendary: those who perform well in an area of expertise are promoted to supervise others. Thus, they have moved out of doing what they are good at and moved into doing something for which they are often unprepared and unskilled. Institutions often do not address this dilemma, and professional associations can fill the gap. For example, Wood and Kia describe the active role played by

NAFSA: Association of International Educators in the professional development of international student advisors. This association has identified professional standards and competencies, promulgates a code of ethics, and provides leadership training and development.

The associations cited in the chapters and listed in the Appendix are key to the professionalism and legitimacy of these administrative areas. Each of these areas represents a unique field of practice that must conduct research and writing to develop a knowledge base, sponsor journals and publications to disseminate the knowledge, establish professional codes of conduct, and provide education and training to enable their members to increase their skills and advance their careers. According to these authors, it seems that the professional associations are least adept at supporting the research and writing needed to advance their fields. Only Olsen, in the institutional research (IR) arena, speaks to the solid contribution of research and, given the skills and orientation of those in IR, this seems natural. Rosser observes in her literature review that case studies particular to functions or regions are more available than national studies of midlevel administrators as a group. Nonetheless, these authors suggest that more is needed and cite a number of potential topics ripe for study.

The purpose of this volume has been to profile the careers of a number of midlevel administrators and demonstrate the high degree of talent and expertise that is evident among them. We hope that we have inspired those outside of these administrative units to consider these positions as viable career options. We also hope that we have inspired those within these units to consider advancing their own career or their profession by becoming more active in an association or launching a study to contribute to the knowledge base of their field. As Rosser indicates, midlevel administrators may well be the unsung professionals in higher education, but the authors of these chapters describe roles and responsibilities that are critical to the quality and vitality of the academic enterprise.

Appendix. Professional Associations, Journals, Publications, and Web Sites

Position	Associations	Journals/Publications	Web Sites
Academic advising	National Academic Advising Association (NACADA)	National Academic Advising Association Journal	http://www.ksu.edu/nacada/
Institutional advancement	Council for Advancement and Support of Education (CASE)	Currents	http://www.case.org
	National Society of Fund Raising Executives (NSFRE)	Advancing Philanthropy Code of Ethical Principles and Standards of Practice	http://www.nsfre.org/
	Association for Research on Nonprofit Organizations and Voluntary Action (ARNOVA)	Nonprofit and Voluntary Sector Quarterly	http://www.arnova.org
	Public Relations Society of America (PRSA)	Public Relations Tactics, The Strategist	http://www.prsa.org/
Information technology	EDUCAUSE (CAUSE and EDUCOM were consolidated to create EDUCAUSE.)	EDUCAUSE Review EDUCAUSE Quarterly	http://www.educause.edu/
Human resources	College and University Personnel Association (CUPA)	CUPA Journal	http://www.cupa.org/

Appendix. (continued)

Position	Associations	Journals/Publications	Web Sites
International student affairs	Association of International Educators (NAFSA)	International Educator	http://www.nafsa.org/
	American Association of Collegiate Registrars and Admissions Officers (AACRAO)	College and University	http://www.aacrao.com/
	Institute of International Education (IIE)	Open Doors	http://www.iie.org/
	Teachers of English to Speakers of Other Languages (TESOL)	TESOL Journal TESOL Quarterly	http://www.tesol.edu/
	Association of International Education Administrators (AIEA)	Guidelines for International Education at U.S. Colleges and Universities	http://www.aieaworld.org
Enrollment management	American Association of Collegiate Registrars and Admissions Officers (ACCRAO)	College and University	http://www.aacrao.com/
	National Association for College Admissions Counselors (NACAC)	The Journal of College Admission	http://www.nacac.com/index.html
	National Association of Student Financial Aid Administrators (NASFAA)	Journal of Student Financial Aid	http://www.nasfaa.org/
	Council for Advancement and Support of Education (CASE)	Currents	http://www.case.org
	National Orientation Directors Association (NODA)	Journal of Student Orientation and Transition	http://www.wsu.edu/~wsuorien/noda.html
Budget and planning	The Society for College and University Planning (SCUP)	Planning for Higher Education	http://www.scup.org/
	National Association of College and University Business Officers (NACUBO)	Business Officer	http://www.nacubo.org/
	Association for Institutional Research (AIR)	Research in Higher Education	http://www.airweb.org/

Appendix. *(continued)*

Position	Associations	Journals/Publications	Web Sites
Student life and development	National Association for Campus Activities (NACA)	Programming	http://www.naca.org/
	Association of College Unions International (ACUI)	College Unions at Work—Monograph Series	http://www.indiana.edu/~acui/
	Student Affairs Administrators in Higher Education (NASPA)	NASPA Journal: The Journal of Student Affairs Administration, Research, and Practice	http://www.naspa.org/
	American College Personnel Association (ACPA)	Journal of College Student Development	http://www.acpa.nche.edu/
	Association of College and University Housing Officers-International (ACUHO-1)	Journal of College and University Student Housing	http://www.acuho.ohio-state.edu/
Academic business affairs	National Association of College and University Business Officers (NACUBO)	Business Officer	http://www.nacubo.org/
	College and University Personnel Association (CUPA)	CUPA Journal	http://www.cupa.org/
Institutional research	Association for Institutional Researchers (AIR)	Research in Higher Education New Directions for Institutional Research	http://www.airweb.org/
	The Society for College and University Planning (SCUP)	Planning for Higher Education	http://www.nacubo.org/
	Association for the Study of Higher Education (ASHE)	Review in Higher Education	http://www.coe.missouri.edu/~ashe/
	American Educational Research Association–Division J–Postsecondary (AERA-J)	Educational Researcher American Educational Research Journal	http://www.aera.net/

INDEX

Back Issue/Subscription Order Form

Copy or detach and send to:

Jossey-Bass Inc., 350 Sansome Street, San Francisco CA 94104-1342

Call or fax toll free!

Phone 888-378-2537 6AM–5PM PST; Fax 800-605-2665

Back issues: Please send me the following issues at $23 each.

(Important: please include series initials and issue number, such as HE90.)

1. HE _____

_____

_____

$ _____ Total for single issues

$ _____ Shipping charges (for single issues *only;* subscriptions are exempt from shipping charges): Up to $30, add $5^{50} • $30^{01}–$50, add $6^{50} $50^{01}–$75, add $8 • $75^{01}–$100, add $10 • $100^{01}–$150, add $12 Over $150, call for shipping charge.

Subscriptions Please ❑ start ❑ renew my subscription to *New Directions for Higher Education* for the year _____ at the following rate:

U.S.   ❑ Individual $58   ❑ Institutional $104
Canada: ❑ Individual $83   ❑ Institutional $129
All Others: ❑ Individual $88   ❑ Institutional $134

NOTE: Subscriptions are quarterly, and are for the calendar year only. Subscriptions begin with the Spring issue of the year indicated above.

$ _____ Total single issues and subscriptions (Add appropriate sales tax for your state for single issue orders. No sales tax on U.S. subscriptions. Canadian residents, add GST for subscriptions and single issues.)

❑ Payment enclosed (U.S. check or money order only)

❑ VISA, MC, AmEx, Discover Card # _____ Exp. date _____

Signature _____ Day phone _____

❑ Bill me (U.S. institutional orders only. Purchase order required.)

Purchase order # _____

Federal Tax ID 135593032   GST 89102-8052

Name _____

Address _____

_____

Phone _____ E-mail _____

For more information about Jossey-Bass, visit our Web site at:

www.josseybass.com   **PRIORITY CODE = ND1**